T0035499

I FINALLY BOUGHT SOME JORDANS

I FINALLY BOUGHT SOME JORDANS

ESSAYS

MICHAEL ARCENEAUX

HarperOne
An Imprint of HarperCollinsPublishers

I FINALLY BOUGHT SOME JORDANS. Copyright © 2024 by Michael Arceneaux. All rights reserved. Printed in the United States of America. No part of this book may be used or reproduced in any manner whatsoever without written permission except in the case of brief quotations embodied in critical articles and reviews. For information, address HarperCollins Publishers, 195 Broadway, New York, NY 10007.

HarperCollins books may be purchased for educational, business, or sales promotional use. For information, please email the Special Markets Department at SPsales@harpercollins.com.

FIRST EDITION

Designed by Janet Evans-Scanlon

Library of Congress Cataloging-in-Publication Data has been applied for.

ISBN 978-0-06-314041-7

24 25 26 27 28 LBC 5 4 3 2 1

To millennials struggling with aging:

stretch and believe in yourself.

This book is dedicated in loving memory of my mother.

Mama, I am so happy and grateful to be your son.

I love and miss you so much.

Appropriate? Not really. But it's me, and I can't help it.

—*Mariah Carey*

CONTENTS

PLEASE UNBLOCK ME, TONI BRAXTON

This is Michael Arceneaux. He *hates* me."

Don Lemon placed his arm around me as he said this to the small group I was speaking with near the bar.

We were at the inaugural Native Son Awards ceremony at the Cadillac House in Manhattan. Native Son is an intergenerational movement, community, and platform created to inspire and empower gay/queer Black men. It was founded by former *VIBE* editor in chief Emil Wilbekin.

Don was one of the night's honorees.

Feeling empowered, I smiled at Don and replied, "Here you go. . . . Don't you start no shit."

We both laughed, and I proceeded to mention a mutual friend between us to ensure the mood stayed pleasant.

I *try* to play nice with people generally—even when met with small, albeit amusing, provocations.

This was technically the second time he and I had met. The first was at a SiriusXM studio, where we each were guests on the radio show *Bevelations*, hosted by Bevy Smith. At the time, all we did was acknowledge each other's existence. Not so much a direct hello. It was more like a nod—the kind Black men unfamiliar with each other make when in passing, notably in spaces where a lot of us are not around.

I wondered then if he knew who I was and what I had written about him.

I don't assume people—much less of those of his status—know who I am or care what I have to say.

In hindsight, perhaps he did know and ignored me accordingly. Good for him.

And oh well.

I don't hate Don Lemon. He was very entertaining for years on CNN's New Year's Eve specials when he was drunk and full of joy. Of all my critiques about the recent waves of rampant consolidation in media and entertainment, chief among them is that CNN's new owners not only felt compelled to chase after Republican viewers who will never abandon their conservative media ecosystem, but that they took away Don's drinking on the job on NYE. Media objectivity does not exist, and drunk Don Lemon was great television.

Also: his hairline and skin-care regiment only impress me more as time moves on and my age goes up.

Years prior to all of this, however, Don Lemon used to routinely draw controversy with his on-air lecturing—namely to Black folks.

How Black men needed to pull up their pants and abandon sagging. How we needed to "stop using the N-word," "finish school," and "respect where you live." When it came to "respect," he was referencing Harlem, where we both lived at the time, and the apparent large amount of trash around.

I find NYC to be filthy generally, too, but some neighborhoods are noticeably cleaner than others for reasons that have mainly nothing to do with the individual cleanliness of the neighborhood residents, but which neighborhoods are prioritized by the people who run sanitation services and why. There were other comments he made, and though I didn't hate Don Lemon personally, his harangues did irk the hell out of me.

And with my main work consisting of writing about public figures and issues, he was a constant source of content.

Did I write about my feelings in the kindest way?

No, not really, but my point was always that some of us have a responsibility to speak to our own with compassion—especially when given platforms as large as CNN.

After the death of Alton Sterling and Donald Trump's ascension to the presidency, Don Lemon's politics seemingly changed, as did the tone of my work.

At least we could laugh about it . . . now, anyway.

I don't have a problem with directly facing any of the people whom I have criticized in my work, but the further along I have gotten in my career, some have stepped in to alert me that my words can cut deep enough to linger in ways that might hinder me professionally.

A difference of opinion is fine by me, but not everyone feels that way.

I got a call from someone in the entertainment industry worried about how the tone in my writing might impact my career beyond writing on the internet. She was worried about a tweet I had sent, one referencing something I had written about Lee Daniels, criticizing him over comments he made in an interview about Black homophobia.

She didn't tell me not to have an opinion or not to express it, but to be mindful of how I expressed it.

"You're going to be in rooms with these people sooner than you think, Arceneaux."

She was not telling me to abandon all my opinions, but suggested I consider the tone in which I articulated my frustrations with how some people speak or act. You know, before I potentially screw up a potential opportunity—one that could get me out of writing on the internet for the rest of my life. I accept that I was born opinionated and want to express my feelings as I see fit, but I don't necessarily want to make a living primarily writing about them in this dying medium forever.

She knew my greater ambitions, hence the call.

She was the same person that cautioned me against potentially embarrassing myself for crumbs on a reality show some years prior, so I couldn't dismiss her note outright.

I deleted the tweet, but the essay would stay up as long as the site hosting it did.

Shortly after my first book was released, I got an email from the head of Lee Daniels's production company asking about the rights to it.

Shortly before the book was released, my friend Samantha had asked if she could send an advanced copy to her TV agent.

My response was immediate: yes . . . and may God and Beyoncé's light forever shine upon thee.

Jason the agent loved the book and wanted to work with me, but I had to level with him when I told him about the email.

Uh, I definitely wrote some shit about him. So never say never, but let's see how that goes.

I met with Lee while in Los Angeles for my book tour, and separately with Jerrod Carmichael, who was also interested.

And because life is so random, I was asked to try out for some Bravo show while I was in baggage claim. Not a reality show, but a kind of panel show where men spoke about reality TV. I was told nice things about my last-minute audition, though I was ultimately not chosen, but I can confirm that Jerry O'Connell is a nice man who treated me with the sort of kindness I have come to learn is rarer than it should be.

The show in question has already been canceled, but I could have used the check.

As all of this was going on, I was desperately broke and waiting for a late check to pay my late rent. This major conglomerate that owned the publication I wrote for not only "forgot" to process my invoice but also told me that they now had to issue me a paper check—which I had to have shipped to my hotel in order to cash it and avoid an eviction notice.

After the check finally did arrive, I was able to walk into the meetings I actually came to LA for without that anxiety hovering over me.

When an author allows someone to option their work for film rights, they have very little say in the adaptation.

The kind of dramatization often required for Black films to be nominated and awarded could easily be pulled out of my story. But I was not interested in the prospect of an actress my mama didn't like tossing me into a trash can and lighting it on fire as I ultimately grew up to fall in lust with someone who looked like a Spicy White Jesus.

You at least have hope and prayer if you want to write the television adaptation yourself. So I wanted that option.

When I entered the production company's office for the meeting, the first thing I did was do something wrong.

I loved the polite look Lee gave me after I sat in his seat.

Oh, I'm in the rich man's seat. Sorry. My mistake.

Gon' and sit on the commoner couch, Arceneaux.

Lee was incredibly nice—especially when I got my ass out of his chair.

His producing partner was also very nice.

As expected, Lee, an Oscar-nominated director, initially wanted to make a film out of the book, but his producer partner convinced him that a TV show made more sense financially.

For them and for me.

My plan was to mention that I had written critically about him at some point. I felt he had a right to know. I would have liked to know if I were in his position.

Besides, I had already watched people on social media announce they were working with someone whom they had dragged up and down the internet.

My concern was when and how to bring it up. Ultimately, Lee provided the opportunity for me to do so.

My habit of raising my hand to ask if I can ask a question—as if I am in a classroom—has never wavered. It helps speed up the process in situations like these. When Lee brought up the subject of Black people and homophobia, I listened . . . waited . . . and shot my hand up high.

After being called on, I let him know that I had written critically about his remarks on this very subject.

He smiled and asked playfully, "You wrote about me, bitch?"

I smiled back and told him, "I could pull it up right now if you want and send it to you."

I didn't disagree about homophobia's existence in the Black community nor his experience with it. Where I did differ with him was the insistence of its level of pervasiveness as compared to other communities. A lot of the homophobia in Black communities here and abroad can be traced to the contributions from white Evangelicals. Black people get a bad rap because of who is often in control of the narrative.

After I said my piece, spouted a few stats, and explained why I wrote what I did, Lee was receptive, respectful, and engaged.

I don't often get the opportunity to tell people I write about how I feel about something they've done or said, but I try not to waste the chance when it comes.

I noted that this was me, the critic and political writer, speaking, but that I was there to talk about making television.

I found out that he later told the very friend that warned me about my tweets that I was a "doll."

I take it as a great compliment from a Black elder.

I worked with him and Jerrod Carmichael (who, for what it's worth, remembered something nice I wrote about *The Carmichael Show*) together on the adaptation for a few years, but it didn't work out—for no reason related to anything I've written on the internet or tweeted.

I carried that same spirit of full disclosure two years later when I met with execs at Kevin Hart's production company.

That gave me the chance to go back to LA and try to set up my second book somewhere before its release.

It was the last meeting I had before the lockdown.

When my agent told me that Kevin Hart's people were interested, I had to once again offer a disclaimer.

Hey, you know how I told you I was going to stop writing about famous people because you have to get me some TV money? Okay, I definitely made an exception in this case. Damn.

Some editors remember me only when Black men die or when Black men fuck up.

Many felt Kevin Hart did not handle responses to old gay jokes he made—resulting in him bowing out of the Oscars. Kevin Hart is the sort of famous that even white editors at mainstream publications know about, so my inbox became busy with requests for me to write about the situation. My opinion was that he never actually apologized and everyone would benefit if he simply said, "I'm sorry" and moved on.

It took Kevin Hart a long while to reach that same conclusion, however, so the issue dragged out long enough for me to be given multiple assignments to write the same plea.

By the time my agent told me his production company was interested, I had watched his Netflix docuseries and was satisfied that he was not a raging homophobe. I suppose some people know when it's time to post a Notes app apology faster than others.

When I got to the production company's office, I sat in the lobby and checked my email as more meetings I had scheduled were being canceled. It was the beginning of the pandemic, and everyone was starting to realize how serious the situation was. While waiting in the front for my meeting, Kevin Hart entered, shook my hand, and said good morning. I'd been around enough people in that industry to know that this wasn't exactly a guarantee. No wonder he's so rich.

He did not stay for the meeting, but like the other one before it, I went in knowing what I wanted. And by this point, I knew exactly what to say and how, as most of these meetings were all the same.

Like every other one, it was pleasant, and everyone was very nice. Yet, like the Lee situation, this one was special, and I was waiting for the right time to make my disclosure.

This meeting was lovely, but just so y'all know that I'm not a fake-ass bitch, I wrote about Kevin Hart.

They glanced at one another and appeared sort of amused. Turns out, they had already known. Preparation, like eye contact, is not a given with these types, either. Points for preparation.

After my declaration, I was asked if I had watched Kevin's Netflix show.

Yeah, I was cool with it—otherwise I wouldn't have come.

I said it with a smile.

They wanted to work with me.

I'm a critic, but I'm not an asshole.

Unfortunately, not every single time am I able to make such a distinction clear.

✦

Knowing my affinity for Toni Braxton, one of my best friends told me that I needed to listen to her new single. I have been performing the *Toni Braxton* album since the early 1990s, so I was happy to see her back in music. And being the longtime fan that I am, I promptly went to Twitter in order to spread the gospel about it.

As I was trying to offer her free promotion, I realized that Toni Braxton had blocked me.

"How Could an Angel Break My Heart" immediately started playing in my head.

I was trying to stan, only to find out my voice had been silenced by someone I adore.

A block from Toni Braxton is like my childhood flipping me off.

Generally, I believe no one should see anything that they don't want to.

I have blocked antagonistic conservatives, homophobes, hoteps, racists, adults failed by No Child Left Behind, and other annoyances.

Many block me back—including a few public figures.

I couldn't care less if someone like Kenya Moore has me

blocked. I did not enjoy her on *The Real Housewives of Atlanta* until season fourteen. Motherhood looks great on her, but a lot of it had to do with the franchise being so bad that you can't help but appreciate Miss USA. Before that, she made comments here and there that turned me off. She was an effective villain in that way.

I've argued with men who enjoy her and can't believe I feel this way.

I continue to question their taste in people, but for what it's worth, I do enjoy randomly shouting, "Kenya Moore Hair Care."

I don't care what most people think of me unless it impacts my earning potential, and by this time, I had been writing long enough to where I should have been used to it.

But this was different.

It was Toni Braxton.

I LOVE HER.

How could an angel break my heart?

It took me a minute to figure out potential causes.

I frequently used to live-tweet *Braxton Family Values* when it aired on WE tv.

I have long developed a habit of coming up with nicknames for people, and while watching the show, I developed quite a few for Toni's sisters.

I referred to Trina Braxton as "Mountie Braxton" because I had never known a person from Maryland who talked like she was from a province in Quebec. Her voice still sounds stunning on the criminally underappreciated album *So Many Ways*, released in 1996 by The Braxtons (Trina, Towanda, and Tamar). She sounds American, too.

I called Towanda Braxton "Yolanda Adams–Face Braxton." In

my defense, Yolanda Adams is pretty and sanctified. How can it be shade when she is a star for Jesus?

I sometimes called Traci Braxton "Left-Behind Braxton" in reference to her storyline of . . . being left behind on the show. Traci has since passed, but she actually followed me on Twitter. I liked her solo music once it was released, and was happy she got her moment. She, along with her sister Tamar Braxton, were the comedy reliefs, but they each had talent that I was happy to see finally get shown outside of the shadows of their famous sister.

I thought all of this was relatively harmless until I looked at my phone one morning.

The only other comment I could recall that might not have translated as well was the time I did say Toni Braxton was sort of like the Shug Avery of R & B. But who doesn't love Shug Avery? She could control Mister and helped Celie find her freedom.

I said way worse as a teenager/twentysomething on my old blog, which I deleted to avoid situations like this, having to explain the shit I talked to those people who want to pull me out of the hood.

I did not delete my tweets fast enough.

I said way worse about Don Lemon, and look how nice that ended—eventually, anyway.

I have purchased so many Toni Braxton albums—including the ones many of y'all didn't buy, like *More Than a Woman,* which is another criminally underrated album from the Braxton family; *Libra*; and *Pulse.* I also purchased Toni Braxton's duets album with Babyface: *Love, Marriage & Divorce.*

I did not buy *Sex & Cigarettes* because my feelings were hurt, but I did attend the As Long as I Live Tour in support of it. For the record, the Shug Avery analogy was apt. It's not a bad thing! It's not like I called her "Lady Eloise."

I was only cracking jokes, and I ended up banned by one of my all-time favorite artists.

One lesson to draw from this is to stop posting using hashtags.

I try to be respectful of public figures and not @ them on social media in consideration of their feelings, but after Toni Braxton blocked me, I started to avoid using hashtags, too.

I can't control people who search their own names, however.

I participated in a panel centered on the state of R & B, where each of the panelists was also treated to copious amounts of wine onstage during the conversation. Was that the best idea for me, already a highly opinionated person sober? I've never been called a mean drunk, so I figured, *What's the worst that could happen?*

Being blocked by another singer I love.

I can't recall the exact phrasing as the red wine was hitting; I said something to the effect of, *I thought Jhené Aiko didn't have the biggest voice, but she uses the voice she has incredibly well.* It was in response to the likening of Jhené to Sade, who I feel has a fuller voice than some folks often give her credit for.

I take great pride in being a Sade fan since the days of playing her album on a Fisher-Price record player. To me, when newer artists are promoted or touted as the next version of an established artist, it sets them up for a trap very few can ever escape. *Just be you and rest on your own laurels* is all I meant.

Evidently, I phrased the sentiment far differently than intended, because the next day, I got texts and tagged in tweets pointing out how sharp I sounded.

I ignored it the way I ignore plenty of messages, but similar to me wanting to rave about a Toni Braxton song, when I was trying to look at Jhené's page to find a link to her latest single, I noticed that I was blocked.

I know that I said that she doesn't have the biggest voice, but I love Jhené Aiko's music. I find her voice, however apparently I described it, to be soothing. The same goes for her catalog. During the plague, I found her usage of sound bowls on some of the tracks of a then-new album to be especially comforting. So much so that I turned to her sound bowl playlists to help me sleep in the summer of 2020 in Harlem, when the sounds of sirens and fireworks could be heard all night.

For what it's worth, during that time, I realized that whatever I had said about her voice was wrong.

I'm old enough to know better by now not to personalize bullshit on the internet, but for a fan, it's embarrassing to be blocked by the artist you adore. Some people revel in being blocked by anyone famous. I mean, it is funny to read people claim online that they were blocked by singers like Anita Baker for suggesting she duet with Toni Braxton. But I do not enjoy being blocked by Toni Braxton or Jhené Aiko.

I understand that no matter what, I'm not blocked in real life. That all of my pleasant memories related to her music remain intact. That no one can take *Braxton Family Values* clips on YouTube away from me.

Nothing can stop me from cooing like Jhené on *Sail Out*, and I'll continue singing "Sativa" like I wrote it.

The sting lingers all the same, but in the case of Toni Braxton, has mildly subsided after she left Twitter following Elon Musk's acquisition of the company.

As long as she doesn't read this book, she won't block me on Instagram or TikTok.

Should she change her mind or the service is sold to someone less irritating, I have but one plea: Please unblock me, Toni Braxton.

Please don't let me fall.

Don't let it be too late.

I hope Jhené Aiko will unblock me, too.

I believe in the power of forgiveness—especially when the person seeking forgiveness knows your deep cuts.

I continue to make a sizable portion of my income writing my opinions about various topics and public figures, but I will be more mindful of what I say about the artists I'm a fan of. It doesn't mean I can't be critical, but perhaps I'll speak with less bite and more care.

These past couple of years have taught me that I don't edit myself as well as I think I do.

I'm always going to have something to say, but I am trying to figure out in real time when I should speak on something and when to keep my jokes, critiques, and shade in a text.

After all, dummy, people can see what you say on the internet.

Midway through summer 2022, I got a random DM on Instagram from a former cast member of *Love & Hip Hop: Atlanta*. He asked me if I used to write for a gossip blog. I did. It helped me pay loans and was fun if not mindless work, because I wrote about light fare under a pseudonym that, in hindsight, was not a good cover.

"You wrote a story about me that pops up on the first page of Google, and it kills me."

I could not recall the story he was talking about. I lost count of how many articles I have written under my own name several years prior, much less one under a handle. After doing some digging, I realized he was talking about something I may have written all the way back in 2013.

He wasn't on the show for long and had gone on to accomplish a lot that superseded my light dragging over some scene I couldn't even remember anymore.

He wanted to see if I could get rid of the post.

That was out of my control, so I directed him to the site owner.

I did at least say, "Sorry about that, for real."

I didn't hate the man.

I was just talking my shit and trying to make my money.

WHO ALL GON' BE THERE?

When it came to the prospect of a book tour, my main concern was always whether anyone would care to show up.

Much as I appreciated my friends for trying to convince me otherwise at the onset of my first book release, this was very much a valid question to ask. The average American does not consume a lot of books each year. There was also not an overflow of institutional support for someone like me.

Throughout the years it took for me to find an agent and, ultimately, a publisher, I was repeatedly told how niche my story was—hence why my first book tour was largely supported by way of my community, as opposed to the industry on the whole.

The publisher did at least help me find bookstores in different cities to set up events, but financially, I was largely on my own for most of the travel and lodging. That isn't novel to authors—notably first-time ones—but some of us face deeper disadvantages under such circumstances. If not for the help of other Black creatives, executives, friends, and family members, I likely would have been relegated to the one launch event that I had in New York City. That was very well-attended, but I knew enough people in that city to fill the back room of a bookstore. Same for Houston.

It wasn't necessarily a guarantee anywhere else—I only have but so many friends.

As it turns out, quite a few people showed up to events in other cities like Los Angeles, Philadelphia, and Baltimore. All kinds of people, at that. Even a rat made an appearance at one book event.

Right at the beginning of the Q & A portion, the rat in question rushed through the crowd. That prompted immediate screams and spurred most of the audience to run like hell away from the disease-carrying menace. Deeply afraid of rats and mice, I would have absolutely understood if everyone said, "Fuck this," and fled the scene.

I don't do rodents.

Some people who grew up on the East Coast think I am ridiculous to still be afraid of a rat or mouse.

You're from Texas. Y'all have those big-ass roaches. You should be more scared of them.

Well, I *am*, but there are giant flyswatters and machetes to deal with them.

A rat—especially one of those on the East Coast—drinks rat poison like it's strawberry soda and doesn't flinch at most humans, armed or not.

I don't care how big the roaches are in Texas. It doesn't matter that I have to worry about being eaten by an alligator in other states like Florida. I don't do rats and will never, ever get used to their presence. I hope they all die.

Yet at that moment, I couldn't just get up and leave. This event was about my book. I was a first-time author that needed this to go well. I couldn't run without moving more product—and of course, thanking the people for showing up.

This was also an event where the publisher covered my hotel. Rodent terror had filled my soul, but I felt obligated to earn my keep. So I picked my legs up before the rat could get to my ankles, and with mic in hand, I summoned someone to find a python or whatever rat-killing weapon they could muster so we could all continue with the event.

After a few minutes, the rat must've realized that I was not J.K. Rowling or some other ill-willed human they could bond with and scurried away somewhere. Thankfully, most of the audience stayed once it ran back to its preferred circle of hell or wherever. I don't want to identify the bookstore in question, but I will note that the staff there was gracious and incredibly accommodating apart from that mildly hilarious moment with the guest no one invited.

I will say that it was in DC, where rats and black squirrels roam every block in the "urea" as if they own the ground.

I had no idea if folks would come here to talk about the book I wrote, but the fact that so many people came to see me made me both grateful and vindicated. As I repeatedly stressed to doubters in publishing that people, no matter their background, will find my stories relatable and thus as commercially viable as anyone else's, so long as you put them out there. I wanted to prove a point, and rat or not, the room made me feel like I did.

I'm not especially mushy, but there were moments after each event when I tried to take in that people did indeed care about what I had got to say. I had no real measure of what would constitute success for me, but I knew that I didn't share that much of myself to be met with dead silence.

The tour was largely positive as far as showing me subtle progress had been made. As in a country-as-hell me, with my gay-ass stories and complicated views on religion, family, and intimacy, could pull all types of people together in the same room to listen to me read and react. It's not an arena or theater tour, but it's something to be proud of.

The more I kept going—lectures, speaking engagements, other book events—the more I felt people were becoming more accepting in ways I did not grow up experiencing.

Not every event on that tour was a success.

There was one scheduled at my alma mater, Howard University, that was a flop by every metric.

It was scheduled on a Saturday morning, which even at the time felt off. Most of my other events were held during the week and scheduled basically around the time people were off of work. I wasn't even in town for this. I came for a wedding, and the event was a last minute add-on.

I wasn't going to turn down the chance to speak at the college I graduated from.

I spent so many years on that campus wanting to come back for this very moment—a book!—and then, whew, there was an empty room and initially confused staff members.

Hi, I'm Michael. I'm here for the event.

I will never forget the confused look I got in response.

She looked at me as if I had wandered my way in from that McDonald's across the street on Georgia Avenue. I won't deny going there for chicken nuggets when in need, but depending on the hour, the people inside could give *The Walking Dead* vibes. To prove I wasn't lost, I pointed to the poster of me hanging in the Howard University bookstore to the side.

"Oh, oh, oh," she said.

I should have taken that as a cue to flee, but I stayed and hoped my feeling that this was not about to go well would be wrong.

I'm grateful to all three of the people who stopped by—one of whom stumbled along and wished me luck without buying a book (I don't count people's money—and either way, it's okay). It was all kind of funny—in an anticlimactic, somewhat humiliating sort of way. I was back at the same bookstore that I had dreamed of returning to for this very moment, and I was sitting around looking as lost and stupid as I had my first week on campus. (At least I didn't have food poisoning this time.)

But sometimes when things go so wrong, all you can do is laugh and be grateful you're due to join the wedding party at a bar in a short amount of time. And so I did as I went down the stairs to join said wedding party up the block for post–wedding day drinks.

Thankfully, it was the only event I've had thus far to play into my fears of failure.

I've since learned that sometimes it can be better to have two and a half folks interested in wanting to meet you and engage in all aspects of your life explored in your work, as opposed to the small parts of it that make them comfortable.

As a writer, I want to go anywhere my writing is welcomed—especially if you want to pay for it.

This was how I found my way to the Midwest—a region I hadn't experienced until my thirties.

I have met plenty of Midwesterners through college and work, but I never had any reason to travel to the middle of the country until my career presented the opportunity.

Chicago immediately appeared segregated—like every other city and town in America that I have visited—but was much nicer to look at. They do have a lot of rats, too, but at least they behaved themselves at the venue. I now understand deep-dish pizza, albeit only with Lactaid.

When I made it to Milwaukee for a speaking engagement, I

was able to avoid the cheese curds, but regrettably couldn't escape conversations about how racist Milwaukee was, no matter the time, place, or person.

It was 8:46 a.m., and I was only minutes off of a plane.

I greeted the Uber driver, and minutes later, after hearing someone on the radio say something that prompted me to reach for my AirPods, I heard a quip about how Milwaukee is apparently the most segregated city in the country.

I wasn't sure of what to say after that proclamation.

Considering how deeply rooted and entrenched racism is in America, I guess it takes a lot of work to become the leading racist metropolis in the nation, so, uh, way to go, Milwaukee?

Instead of congratulations, I went with a response that acknowledged what was said but did not encourage further conversation.

Wow, that's crazy.

I had to say it six times more before he clocked into me being totally disinterested in solving race relations at the present hour.

No matter who else I spoke with over the course of those two days—an Uber driver, a hotel employee, an event organizer, some local businessperson—each led with how racist Milwaukee was. Why do so many white people over there want to talk about racism? Not even in the South have I had white people casually say to me, "Afternoon. How are you? Would you like to talk about how racist this place is?" Probably because their red hats and bumper stickers say it for them, but still. Making it small talk was perplexing and ultimately tiring.

I'm guessing I was one of the few Black people they could interact with outside of an internet connection, but my advice would be to talk about racism with your kin who make it an issue, not me.

Or at least pay me to participate in your panel.

Thoughts and prayers to all Black Milwaukeeans.

At least when I got to Kansas City, I got to take a partial break from racism to focus on the other societal ill plaguing my life and career: homophobia.

I am keenly aware of the reality that, more likely than not, I will spend the rest of my life facing homophobia in varying capacities. Fine, but if I had to choose between someone calling me a slur or subjecting me to faux niceties, I believe now that the f-word is the better, more succinct route. Perhaps it's vintage of me to think this way, but I find someone talking in circles around me about my sexuality to be much more obnoxious.

I was in Kansas City for an event organized by a nonprofit rooted in the preservation and promotion of what I quickly learned was a vibrant Black creative community in Kansas City.

The organizer was a polite and very classy Black woman—which is exactly why I felt bad that I lost my vape pen in her nice car.

I was wearing these black sweats that were perfect for the airport or any day that ended in Y. They fit nice, but things constantly fell out of the pockets. When we got out of the car, I reached under the seat, trying to find the vape without the host realizing what I had misplaced. Regrettably, my long-ass arms were no match for how far the pen fell. What a horrible time to be "too urban," but beyond that, I was on my best behavior.

Sometimes when you do events like these, you are invited to have dinner with the organizers and—depending on how big the group behind the planning is—their board members, donors, and other names for fancy people of means. Your attendance is not technically required, but if you came all this way to collect money and work, might as well show gratitude and sing for your supper. How much it feels like work depends on the personalities of the people present.

This group of primarily Black folks felt familiar, so it was fine to fellowship with them over—uh, upscale BBQ might be the best way to describe it. There were some other guests present who were paler and not any less polite but, as I kept talking to one of them, obviously not especially comfortable with me nor my point of view.

From my understanding, my host was not part of the nonprofit directly, but she did something else related to the city. I guess the event was done in partnership with wherever she came from.

After she sat next to me for dinner, she told me she would be the moderator for tomorrow's event. I was hoping to speak to the Black woman who invited me, who ultimately shared after I had landed that she found the book through her gay son, who came out to her.

Instead, I got Sally, this white lady, who let me know she read the book, though gave no read one way or another how she felt about it generally.

I did notice her fixation on what I said about Megyn Kelly.

She did not like what I had to say about Megyn Kelly.

She asked me why I felt she was racist.

Because Megyn Kelly says racist things.

Mind you, the chapter she was referencing had more to do with dating and trying to become more comfortable with intimacy.

The invocation of Megyn Kelly was related to me not wanting to fuck with a guy—not due to once facing charges for violently attacking an ex but to vigorously defending Megyn Kelly because he worked with her. And he had the nerve to be Black too!

Anyone who read my first book would know that if I didn't

want to continue dating someone who felt so strongly about that silly person, I likely didn't want to have dinner chatter about it.

But I was on the clock, so I followed with a couple of instances from the book that she claimed to have read.

Sally challenged me about each—preventing me from enjoying the fancy ribs in front of me in peace.

Initially, she seemed polite—almost unusually so—and even somewhat reserved, until we sat down and her passive-aggressiveness took the lead.

So this was that "Midwest nice" shit I'd heard about.

After I successfully fought the urge to roll my eyes at her fourth Megyn Kelly–related question, Sally kind of winced when I made a joke related to my attraction to men.

Suddenly, she was uncomfortable.

Welcome to my world.

Why this Fox News–loving older white woman was placed in charge with talking to me the next morning did not quite connect.

And that same Megyn Kelly Forever energy carried over the next day at the event.

This was the first book-related event I had done where the person did not ask me anything about the book itself.

Sally had plenty of questions about my writing—but most of them were related to the political commentary and cultural criticism I had published online through the years before my book was published. She even dug up old blog posts I thought had been wiped from the internet. She reminded me of the conservatives that sometimes email me with the hopes of baiting me into a back-and-forth.

Even people whom I can tell have not read my books have managed to ask me questions about *aspects* of it.

You gay, right? And you love your mama? Something about fleas and Jesus?

All of her questions curiously avoided most of the themes of my book—especially about my sexuality. Perhaps I'm stereotyping Sally, this Fox News–loving older white woman, but it sure felt like me writing about my sexuality and having select opinions about religion and race made her very uncomfortable.

Again, I have no idea why she was the moderator, but the event organizer got visibly frustrated and ultimately grabbed the audience microphone and redirected questions to the book.

It immediately got better once I could engage with her and the crowd in the way I had hoped to.

I don't hold the organization that invited me accountable for my exchange with Sally, but I do feel people like her need to be challenged on what informs their discomfort. She didn't give me the chance. Polite as Sally was, a better show of etiquette would have been to ask me about my book at a book event centered on my book. Regardless, the event ended on a better note once I diverted my attention away from her. Just about everyone else there was great.

Once the Q & A and book signing wrapped, I stuck around to take a few pictures with attendees—including one who felt me up while taking a picture with me.

I held my composure in spite of that violation. I'm proud of myself for that. Violence is not the answer, but not respecting someone's personal space and agency may get you popped. It was too red in this region to play with that; I chose to politely shove him away with a smile after the photo was taken.

As grateful as I am to anyone spending their time and money on something written by me, please don't reach for my ass. This book was a paperback release. You have already supported me at a lower price point. Have you not gotten enough of a deal already?

Inappropriate as that was, the moderator bothered me more all the same.

Much as I don't want people touching me without permission, at least the creep wasn't bothered by my gay material.

Perhaps that moderator was an up-close-and-personal preview to the sort of mindset behind legislation like Florida's "Don't Say Gay" Bill, which has since been repurposed by other GOP-controlled states across the country. Or the ongoing targeting of libraries across the country over the inclusion of books that cover topics like racism, sexuality, and gender, led by organizations like Moms for Liberty—a group best categorized as the Daughters of the Confederacy for the digital age. All of them do this under the pretense of "parental rights," but it's vintage prejudice from the usual suspects.

There has been pushback, but not enough to ease my worry about what the future will look like as those who wince about my sexuality now garner more legislative cosigns.

Such concerns won't stop me from writing and wanting to connect with people. I'm not going to stop being gay or writing about how awful know-nothing people make what should be trivial an apparent lifelong headache.

The pandemic wouldn't allow me to tour for my second book. Zoom and IG Lives aren't the worst thing, but they're not the same as in-person events. I'm looking forward to trying it again now that it's relatively safer.

As nice as it can be to get flown out and put up to talk about your art, I want to meet readers who appreciate my worth as a writer—preferably readers who can keep their unwanted hands and views to themselves.

SIT BACK AND ENJOY THE TROLL

I have never felt more bougie in my life," Sarah, my friend of over fifteen years, said to me after leaving the Warner Theatre in Washington, DC.

We had bonded as Howard University students over a shared love of catfish, Project Pat, and twerking to Beyoncé's *B'Day* album at Club Love (RIP).

My visits to DC have become infrequent, but one constant remains no matter when I'm there: it always trips me up how DC looks less like the version that I remember.

So much of the new construction makes the city look more homogeneous, and its inhabitants noticeably less Black.

I felt like I was going to fall out of the car the first time I spotted a white woman running on Georgia Avenue.

Sarah had agreed to come with me for the purpose of my trip: to witness *Set It Off: Live on Stage*, a theatrical adaptation of the 1996 cult-classic film directed by F. Gary Gray that starred Queen Latifah, Jada Pinkett Smith, Vivica A. Fox, and Kimberly Elise.

I wouldn't say Sarah was being "bougie" for being somewhat perplexed at how much the sold-out crowd salivated over this messy spin of the beloved film. I wasn't surprised by that. I was not expecting metal detectors, but the clips of the play I had found on Twitter and YouTube helped me measure my expectations.

I was there to review the play for *The Root*—fully expecting a spectacle.

Sarah went in blindly.

Let me start off with the things that I enjoyed about *Set It Off: Live on Stage*. I appreciate the fact that it started at around 3:15-ish versus the appointed time, 3:00 p.m., printed on our tickets. It could have been much later. Not to stereotype any more than the venue's management for making the audience go through metal detectors before being seated, but a lot of Black folks are late to these plays. It's a shame that I had already consumed some wings with my cherished mumbo sauce before showing up to the theater, because there was some noticeably well-seasoned chicken being served in the theater lobby that you could smell from the inside.

The person behind *Set It Off: Live on Stage*, Je'Caryous Johnson, is a native Houstonian. In theory, the casting was technically pretty good, as far as aesthetics go. The rapper turned television personality Da Brat played the role of Cleo, originally played by Queen Latifah. That made all the sense in the world. The same went for LeToya Luckett, a former member of Destiny's Child, who, thanks to her haircut at the time, was the perfect fit for the role of Frankie. I'm sure Vivica A. Fox, who originally played Frankie, would have approved. The actress Kyla Pratt from *One on One* fame was Stony, the character originally played by Pinkett Smith. Then there was Demetria McKinney, whose time on *The Real Housewives of Atlanta* was about as long as this sentence, rounding out the cast as T.T., Elise's character.

It was a respectable cast for a stage play version of a film that no one had really asked for.

The problem, however, was that not all of them seemed to be acting in the same play.

LeToya Luckett was acting within the realm of a classy Southern drama that aired on a network like OWN—think the Ava DuVernay–helmed *Queen Sugar*. I adore LeToya Luckett because her solo material is of the same quality as the earliest Destiny's Child albums and she's from the same hood as me. I regret not yelling, "HIRAM CLARKE HO!" during the play at some point while she was acting, paying homage to my high school alma mater. Given LeToya had scored acting roles on HBO, BET, and OWN, she tried very hard to be a serious actress on a not-totally-serious production.

I admired her effort.

Kyla Pratt seemed like she was on, like, a sanctified version of the show *Empire*, which actually makes me think of another OWN drama, *Greenleaf*. I'm happy you can stream old episodes of *One on One*, but I would like to see Kyla Pratt more often—and with more challenging material.

Demetria McKinney was on one of Tyler Perry's scripted shows that aired on TBS and used a laugh track. The best part about her was how often she tried to work in the fact that she could sing every chance she got.

I couldn't quite peg what kind of show Da Brat was coming from; let's say she was being herself, but it was lovely to see her. I used to be obsessed with "Funkdafied" and "Give It 2 U." Out of nowhere, she started rapping her lines and then proceeded to perform her verse from Lil' Kim's "Not Tonight (Ladies Night Remix)."

That was how we went into intermission. What did that song have to do with the play? Nothing, but everyone seemed happy she brought up one of the hits.

The play relied heavily on the original dialogue, but there were some noticeable shifts. These made it confusing, as they jumped from nineties references to an arguably unneeded invocation of Black Lives Matter–themed dialogue. It's not that police brutality hasn't always been an issue worth addressing, but some language used now wasn't back then. I don't like dialogue that reminds me of a think piece.

Still, that made more sense than the inclusion of ghosts.

In those moments, I was happy Sarah and I hit the vape before we met the spirits.

I guess what made my friend feel somewhat bougie was that at the end of the play, the director gave a speech thanking the crowd for its support but proceeded to brand the production "Black Broadway." That comment had me recalling that he referenced Nelson Mandela *in the press release for this play*.

I whispered to Sarah, "Nigga, this is not August Wilson."

It was a sold-out crowd of happy, entertained Black people. Johnson had every reason to be proud of himself, but wasn't Mandela enough?

But who am I to deny Johnson for being proud of himself?

And he made the crowd happy.

I must admit that I chopped the play up in my review, but I did make note of that and encouraged people to see it if it was in their city.

I would take myself less seriously given the circumstances, but in fairness, what I saw on Broadway about a year or so later was not any less unserious, though critically lauded.

I don't remember who first asked me if I was going to see *Slave Play*, but it was certainly someone who didn't know me well.

The playwright, Jeremy O. Harris, was someone *described by* Out *magazine* as "the queer Black savior the theater world needs."

Many critics at the time offered a similarly glowing appraisal, but this did not garner interest in the play to me. I skipped the night designated for Black attendants. I read that the play was about three interracial couples that attend a multiday retreat where they seek to treat their intimacy issues through a fictional therapeutic method created by a Black psychologist and her white partner called "Antebellum Sexual Performance Therapy." In the play, this is designed to treat sexual *anhedonia*—the inability to feel pleasure.

The practice is essentially BDSM meets slavery.

I don't root for the failure of Black creatives, but I did not want to spend *my* money on that.

I only knew of Harris through an essay he had penned years prior *called* "Decolonizing My Desire." The first line of it went as follows: "I can place the exact moment when white bodies colonized my subconscious, and when blue-eyed men with sun-kissed arms began to hold my desires upon their shoulders like Atlas."

Every artist has a right to explore whatever subject matter they so desire, but that is not my kink. In one respect, I was happy for a young gay Black playwright's success, but some spectacles are more easily digestible to me than others.

I did end up seeing the play months later at the invitation of another friend, Ashley. She was the perfect person to see it with. Because not only was she one of the smartest, kindest people I had met in the media while in New York, but she understood my background and perspective in ways most in the media could not.

And apparently, I had a good date, too.

I was not bringing my white husband with me to see this.

I laughed and nodded along with her.

After accepting her invitation to go, I decided to shy away from my skepticism and leave open the possibility that I might enjoy the play.

Minutes into the start of the play, I let that option expire.

I didn't go into the theater planning to view it through the lens of a cultural critic. I wanted to suspend that part of my brain and try to enjoy the production and its provocations as designed. Yet I found it very difficult to do that over the course of two hours.

To the credit of Harris, it makes you think. Much of what I thought throughout the play was, *What the fuck?*

It opens with Kaneisha, dressed like Mammy in *Gone with the Wind,* twerking to Rihanna's "Work" before going on to eat cantaloupe off the floor to arouse Jim, her white husband playing the role of an overseer named Mista Jim.

I understood going in that this would be unlike any previous Broadway experience I had encountered before, given the subject matter and that the play was intended to be viewed as satire.

I struggled to chuckle along as the therapy these couples participated in involved rape, mammy costumes, the roles of indentured servant and overseer, literal bootlicking, and the word "nigger." You hear phrases like "nasty Negress" and "mulatto" from other characters and see imagery such as a Black man being sodomized by a large Black dildo.

The only one in any real pain was me, though—and perhaps that couple I saw storm out of the theater in disgust.

In the play, Kaneisha says, "The elders don't care that you are a demon; they lay with them too . . . they just want you to know it," in reference to her interracial relationship with a white man.

Much of her dialogue and scenes—including one involving rape—confirmed that I was not the target audience. I found Harris's deployment of sex unsettling. It is not a sensitivity related to my own experience with assault.

Most of the audience, overwhelmingly white, laughed a whole lot throughout the two-hour play (with no intermission).

I didn't say much while watching; my face said enough for me.

I left that theater thankful the experience was over.

After the play, I headed back uptown and stopped at the Whole Foods on 125th Street.

Inside the store, a friend named Mary spotted me with the playbill and asked what I thought of it.

The play has been hailed as "*provocative*" and described as a "*funny, scalding, walk* along the boundary between black and white in America."

A lot of white critics award Black artists who present our pain in this way. I wonder if many of them laughed at the parts not designed to be funny the way the majority white audience in this room did. The play, of course, went on to break the record for the most Tony Award nominations in history.

Not as impressed, I told Mary that I felt it was loud, with nothing to say. Not to me anyway.

I don't know what it's like to be in the position in which "white bodies colonized my subconscious," and those that do have every right to work that out however they choose. As an artist, I can appreciate the vulnerability found throughout the play and the strong performances of the actors involved in helping bring life to this story. And to his credit, Harris brought a lot of Black people to the theater. Others have since followed.

In all sincerity, good for him.

Still, I have never found slavery that funny, and I never want to be in a room of white people who are happy they were given the freedom to feel otherwise.

Whereas my friend Sarah worried over whether she was being a bit highfalutin for not laughing along with the crowd to a chitlin circuit adaptation of a popular 1990s Black movie starring reality stars, rappers, and singers, I sat there on Broadway uncomfortable with white people laughing at us and one person's interpretation of how Black people deal with pain related to white supremacy.

I'm not convinced seeing *Slave Play* in a room full of Black people would have made it any better—even with a comped ticket—but I can say with confidence that seeing it with mostly white people certainly did not help.

It wasn't that they laughed constantly. It's that these white people laughed at the parts that were not funny. There is humor in the play, but not in the microaggressions being chronicled nor the more direct, painful aspects of racism. Where they should have found discomfort, guilt, shame, or regret, they laughed their asses off.

The audience had a good hearty chuckle at the Black woman onstage in her pursuit of racial denigration—for reasons that the play never quite explained in ways for me to understand.

I'm not inclined to give white people any power over me, but it was uncomfortable watching this white audience find such amusement in the desperation of these Black people who can only define themselves through their white romantic partners.

Slave Play has every right to exist. There is no singular way to depict Black people or racism or slavery. And Harris's success has begotten the success of other Black storytellers on Broadway whose work I can better relate to. Designated nights for Black theatergoers or not in its runs, though, the play placated the white gaze.

But in the same way Sarah felt "bougie" for feeling much different about a silly stage play spin on *Set It Off* featuring a legendary stud, I felt like I lived on a different planet than the few Black people in the media who raved about *Slave Play* to me.

Some jokes and plenty of inconsistent opinions on race were being worked out in a play that largely felt provocative for provocation's sake.

I haven't been inside of a theater since the pandemic started.

I received an invitation to see *Slave Play* again once I moved to Los Angeles.

I politely declined. I would rather watch my own cremation than experience that again.

As for the playwright behind the *Set It Off* stage play, he returned with a stage play version of *New Jack City*, starring much of the original cast.

I didn't make it out for that, either.

I GET FADES TO FEEL ALIVE

Yo, Mike, I'm still cutting. I can't not make no money."

It was only week two under lockdown, and my barber was already parked right up the block, cutting hair in his bus on the low.

I didn't fault him for breaking the ordinance. As a fellow free-lancer, I understood that Governor Andrew Cuomo's rules were not going to pay anyone's bills. Many people weren't following the rules, but at least his rule-breaking was rooted in trying to earn a living.

The barbers at his old shop laughed in his face when he first mentioned having the idea to transform a small bus into a barber-shop on wheels.

He had numerous ideas on how to best boost his barber career and, beyond that, maintained several other side hustles. In addition to cutting hair, he shot and edited videos for very local rappers and artists. He managed a few, too, including one he had an on-again, off-again relationship with. He also sold clothes some-times. And weed.

I don't know how some casting agent hasn't discovered him.

"I need to make money" was something he said often when he cut me.

I found him quite relatable in that way.

But when he came up with the idea to run his shop from an old school bus so that he could potentially expand his clientele (and also avoid paying booth rent in someone else's shop), the other barbers tried to clown him over it.

When I first saw the bus, it was parked around the shop he worked in at the time. I didn't immediately see the vision. I went inside at his invitation, and it needed a lot of work. However, I would follow him once he eventually set up his shop on wheels.

He said I was his most loyal client, but that felt like a line on par with what he told some of his girlfriends.

Granted, we did have history by that point, as I am particular about my hair.

My hair started to thin in my twenties—far sooner than I would have liked. Some of it was genetics—beyond my control—but a lot of it was stress and the medication I used to combat that stress. Another big share of fault also went to some incredibly bad barbers.

My Harlem barber with the multiple hustles is the reason I was able to feel good about my hair again.

We were able to get my hairline back on track—or at least as much as God would allow without me traveling to Turkey for surgery.

He did play me about my hair a few times before and after that process, though.

In that same shop where he envisioned a school bus being transformed into a fademobile, he once suggested that I get Beijing hair dye.

I have forgiven but never forgotten that slight. No offense

intended to current participants in that particular style, but I, respectfully, don't like the idea of my scalp resembling an oil spill. When I said no to that, he asked if he could test other "enhancements" on me.

Me: "So you want to test spray paint on me?"

Him: "C'mon, Mike, I need to practice. I'm trying to elevate."

I felt like he used me as a project in his self-taught barber grad school from time to time, but I sometimes allowed him to try his sorcery on me. After that, I would immediately go wash it out at home. Not that it looked bad per se, but if I have to worry about rain or sweat, that's not for me.

He once took it too far when he randomly asked if I could be the test model for a weave installation.

There was a YouTube video playing in front of me at the time. In the video, a barber is doing a step-by-step process of a weave installation. I assumed my barber was kidding until he said he was thinking of another new revenue stream.

Then he gave me that look.

"C'mon, Mike."

It is hard to find a barber who will make your hairline great again and not be a homophobe, so I tried to be supportive, but fuck no.

Again, no disrespect to those who partake in the process. I have no issue with men getting bundles and reimagining them into fades and all that.

Based on the videos that I have seen, it's impressive witchcraft.

Try to cast that spell on someone else's head.

As I said, some parts have thinned, but damn, my hairline never looked bad enough to warrant an inquiry about my interest in a weave.

This is a sensitive subject matter.

Everyone should know their audience.

He saw how my face twisted and took it back.

I actually stopped going to him for a couple of months.

Not out of being offended over the proposed hair tricks, but for the same reason many folks leave their barbers: you get tired of chasing them.

I came home some months later when he spotted me on the street and yelled, "Yo, Mike! Where you been?"

Then he looked at my head and asked, "Who did that to you?"

The answer was some other barber in Harlem I found who could be on time for their appointments but, in retrospect, still had a ways to go on mastering hairlines—mine, anyway.

I had to make peace with his lateness for the sake of appearances.

By then, his bus was up and running, and because he was now parked closer to me, his tardiness was a lot more tolerable.

I went back to getting more compliments about my cuts soon after.

Then the plague came along, and I worried about his business and my scalp.

I'm glad I didn't have to worry for long.

I didn't go immediately once he sent that text, but after walking by him enough for about two weeks when going to the bodega, I gave in.

If I had to pick a sin, it would be vanity.

No wonder I gave into temptation so quickly and so easily.

He couldn't wait to remind me of all of this when I got in the chair—and revel in the moment that he was now getting texts from those "same goofy-ass niggas" trying to use the bus to cut heads when he took off.

I wore a mask every single time I went for a cut.

I read that if you are exposed to COVID in open spaces, try to keep it under twenty minutes. I convinced myself that if I was potentially exposing myself to the virus in that space, it was more like COVID sprinkles versus the whole entree.

He kept the windows open, which provided some nominal comfort in a dicey situation.

My barber laughed at me the first couple of visits. I told him that I didn't know where he was breathing, who was breathing around him, and what all of that breath might do to me.

I would only take my mask off in order for him to trim my goatee. If I'm going to risk my health for the sake of vanity, I may as well fully commit to it. So gon' and line that up, too.

Much as I liked my barber, he was one of those people misinformation campaigns are made for.

He was not a flat-out COVID denier, but he did babble a little bit about the government. He, like a lot of Black folks, rightfully had a reason to distrust the government. But he, like so many Black men I meet in the barbershops, don't have much in the way of media literacy and don't read enough generally.

So, as I explained to him, worry less about the conspiracies that sound far-fetched and focus on the reality that in the United States of America, the government will let us, Black people, die during good times.

Imagine them during a plague where the air is unsafe.

I am not saying that while wearing a tinfoil; I'm reacting to what I read about the Trump administration's handling of the pandemic and saw with my own eyes.

He told me I should be on the news.

I told him to open the window a lil' bit more since he wasn't ready to hear me.

After not taking the virus seriously, by my fourth plague cut, I noticed he had on a mask and had the window popped open a wee bit more.

Like with others, it took someone close to him to be infected in order to understand that not only is the virus a real issue, but it could creep on you.

I was never able to confirm it at the time, but I think I had my brush with the 19 right before it officially swept the globe and spawned the shutdowns.

After traveling back from Houston, my sister was briefly hospitalized for a respiratory issue, and in the weeks after, we all had some version of what we thought was the flu.

I had a fever that lasted for two days that made me feel like I was going to die at select points before it finally broke. And I did have a shortness of breath that lingered for a few weeks. I distinctly remember being at the gym and trying to do my first full-out workout in a while and being so spooked by a sudden but intense shortness of breath that I put those weights back and rushed home.

Even with that fear in the back of my mind, I still wanted to get fades under lockdown.

I don't usually talk much when he cuts me, but when I sat in his chair the first time during the lockdown, I mentioned how much I appreciated that, regardless of what was going on right now, neither of us was trying to fail. We had to make money. We had to be successful.

By the time my second book was released, most of the outside—including bookstores—was closed. Major retailers like Amazon were rightfully shipping medications and essentials like diapers and toilet paper over essay collections. This was all understandable, but not the ideal circumstances to launch your second book.

In one form or another, many of us had to produce no matter what was happening outside, but my success on this project was directly tied to outreach and being physically around people.

You can only do so much from within your walls. Moreover, the book was themed around debt and shame, and I knew the people I wanted the book to reach most were being impacted the hardest economically. I understood there were far worse things in life to grapple with at the time than being stuck at home and downloading Zoom to promote my book.

And, to be totally, completely forthright, even before all of this, I was frustrated with some of the people I was working with for the launch.

I didn't want the sophomore jinx, but what can you do?

I was confident in the material, but worried about the process.

I like to get boosts however I can, and more often than not, I can let go of much of what is bothering me at any given moment when I feel good about my line.

I get fades to feel alive.

No matter how bad things get, if I feel my hair is together, I believe more firmly than I can deal with what is thrown at me.

That's why no matter how broke I've been, I find a way to get a fade or, at the very least, a line-up.

My friend Kim once told me, "You work better when you have a fresh cut."

"You're so pretty" is the response someone else gave me when I conveyed this sentiment to them.

I choose to interpret it as a compliment.

I suppose in theory, during this time, it might have been less of a gamble for me to order some clippers online and learn how to cut my own head. My counterpoint to that is that I have a peanut head, and there is a point in life when you accept who you are. In my case, I am a klutz who would require too much trial and error in this process.

One day, when I have time, perhaps I'll take myself to barber college (probably just YouTube), but at this moment, my barber was the only person I needed.

My hairline had been through enough already.

So there we were in the bus, now both masked up and wanting some sense of normalcy without illness.

Once my book was released, I tried to talk to as many people from my apartment as much as humanly possible.

Sometimes interviewers noticed my fresh cut and assumed I knew how to cut my own hair. I can't recall ever responding directly—just a smile and a nod. I don't like to lie. I'm a terrible liar.

I did not want to entertain anyone's potential judgment.

Initially, I did feel guilty about the visits. It was selfish of me to be going out. And illegal, too. Andrew Cuomo imposed large fines on people who did not adhere to social distancing rules.

"It's not about your life," Cuomo *said* at a press conference in Albany that April. "You don't have the right to risk someone else's life."

He continued, "You don't have the right, frankly, to take healthcare staff and people who are literally putting their lives on the line and be cavalier or reckless with them. You just don't have the right."

It would later be revealed that Cuomo hadn't done all that much to assist the most vulnerable in nursing homes, among other sins tied to his behavior as governor, and he resigned in disgrace.

Good riddance.

But hypocrisy didn't translate to immediate guiltless pleasures for me.

I believe in self-care, but I had to be convinced that what I needed individually mattered enough.

Self-care is done with the intent of caring for yourself, but if the impact potentially harms or takes from others, it's selfishness with better branding. I didn't want my boost to be at the detriment of someone else. I wanted to replenish myself without depleting another.

So I tried to keep to myself.

I would go for runs.

I would eat my feelings.

I worked, and worked, and worked.

I danced at home. I watched too much TV. I doomscrolled the internet for hours on end.

I did the best I could, but nothing helped me escape the turmoil around me and how it impacted me.

Shallow as it sounds, I decided that when the world was on fire, I was offered a vanity boost when I needed it, and took it . . . eventually.

If it's anything, I didn't take trips, cough on elders, or throw all caution to the wind. Whenever I did get a cut, I just went back home and continued to work away and promote.

It was selfish of me, but after scrolling through Instagram Stories enough in the subsequent weeks, I got over it—notably when I saw someone I knew who had gotten COVID POST HIMSELF ON AN AMTRAK TRAIN WITH NO MASK ON.

Clearly, my self-care methodology could be far more selfish and dangerous.

If I hadn't been alone, perhaps I might have moved differently. I might have grown an Afro and revisited looking like Huey Freeman from *The Boondocks* or very slowly learned how to cut my own hair.

I'll weigh my options accordingly for the next plague, but know this: when living in a time of great turmoil, I will do my part for the greater good.

Still, as much as I want to survive, I have to feel alive.

And if I can safely get a fade, I will find a way.

DMJ

Heyyyyy, Michael."

It may sound nice on the surface, but this woman is a menace. This is the same person who constantly interrupts my sleep on any given night because of her hobby of howling at her boyfriend for hours on end. When someone wakes you up that often and for that long, there is only one real reaction to her greeting.

Girl, get the fuck out of my face.

I am sadly too polite to say something like that unless seriously provoked.

I don't have time to bicker with someone for hours on end, anyway. That doesn't mean we have to chitchat, either. I would ignore her altogether had she not learned my name the first time she bugged me to let her into the building when she "lost her key."

"I can't believe I lost it."

Mmhmm.

My neighbor, her boyfriend, had probably put her out.

Again.

During one of her many revelatory three-a.m.-on-a-weekday

shouting expeditions, I learned that his name was on the lease, not hers.

Following that episode, every so often, I would hear her shout "Michael" over and over again, accompanied with a not-so-gentle tap on my window.

Each time I opened the door for this loud-ass woman, I saw it as punishment for not getting someone to install blackout blinds.

I have an expressive face, but I tried to contain it whenever she would disturb me to open the door for her.

I could tell when I sometimes failed because she would say, "I'm so sorry for disturbing you."

A lie proven by my challenged sleep pattern.

I am not that sensitive to noise. I can ignore a lot. You have to when you grow up the way I did. I grew up used to being disturbed by noise that I had no power to tune out. I understood that on any given day, in the middle of the night, a raging alcoholic might be fussing and cussing at maximum volume for extended periods of time. All I could do was hope that perhaps the next day would be calmer and I could catch up on the sleep I missed the night before.

My loud neighbor reminded me of that.

She did that same goofy thing my dad did, where he would rage all night and smile in the morning as if nothing happened. Always a smile, never an "I'm sorry for contributing to the misery-loves-company industrial complex." Even if it wasn't the exact same situation, hearing all of that bickering made me think of other belligerent people who used to disturb my rest.

It was not the sort of memory one cares to revisit, but fortunately, no small children lived in my building.

Only adults who seemingly act like them when disturbed.

I resented her, her man, and their toxic relationship, but the timing and volume of the broadcasting of their problems were the root of my frustrations.

She was so fucking loud. Louder than the cast member from *Black Ink Crew* who used to live upstairs. All the people on *Black Ink Crew* do is fight over dumb shit, drink, and sometimes do tattoos—and then go back to fighting. So the star of that show lived upstairs from me for a time and could maintain quiet hours.

I could always hear her ass.

I could never remember her name, though.

She said it once, but I am not always the best with names. It's been that way since college. I am good with faces, so I can tell you when we met and what we talked about, but the name may take a minute if we don't speak that often.

I'm even worse with the names of people who don't ever let me sleep.

I know her screeches and broken pledges to leave this man.

I know she likes to say at the tippy-top of her lungs, "YOU AIN'T SHIT, NIGGA!"

The only reason I know the name of her man, James, is that sometimes the post office would confuse our units, and I'd get his packages. I tried my best to ignore him outside of that. She did the majority of the screaming, but he's the reason she taps on my damn door.

My rest and her relationship problems were archvillains for years, but I could never recall her name.

When this happens—which is often—I like to come up with a name in my mind for that person instead.

I called her "Drunk Millie Jackson."

Like with the other made-up names I gave people, there was some thought behind it.

Millie Jackson is a soul and R & B singer, one I am several decades removed from.

I know who she is because she appeared on the television show *Martin*, and before that, in my parents' bedroom. My dad owned a vinyl copy of her album *Back to the S**t!*. On the cover of the album, Millie Jackson is sitting on a toilet with a pair of panties down to her ankles, a strained expression on her face.

DMJ was not always all smiles when she needed to be let in. I'm sure it was humbling, if not humiliating, to be dealing with some man who either took away or never gave you a key to his place. So on select days—when it was too hot, too cold, too early, or too late in the day for this bullshit—she had a stank expression on her face. It mirrored the look Millie had on that cover.

Not to mention, based on her weave alone, my neighbor could have been Millie's doppelgänger.

As for the drunk part, some of the times I ran into her or she tapped on my window, she slurred her words in ways unmistakable to someone with firsthand knowledge of what a drunken tongue sounds like. The yelling made more sense once that aspect of her personality became more frequent.

Rude as my nickname sounds, it fits.

Same for the name I gave the neighbor on my floor: Not Maxine Shaw.

She reminded me of the character only if *Maxine Shaw left Kyle Barker and became a hoarder and slight conspiracy theorist.*

Nice woman, but eccentric.

She knocked on my door a lot, too, but at least she kept quiet at night.

I lived in a Harlem brownstone on the first floor. When The Loud One wasn't being put out, she (sometimes?) lived in one of the units on the basement level. The building was gutted into tiny units to capitalize on suckers like me who didn't have many options. It was a mix of old residents and newer people fresh into the city.

When I first moved into this building, it was more like 227 than *Good Times*, but somewhere along the way, there was a slight shift. Initially, I had neighbors like the gay white dude next door or the friendly interracial couple, but that trend only lasted about a year or two of me being there. I'm guessing each of them realized that they could do better.

I deserved better, too, but my private student loans controlled a lot of my life and choices—certainly where I laid my head and for how long.

I needed more time to get ahead of those loans before I felt ready to go through the very long and exhaustive process of finding an apartment in the city.

It was not my ideal apartment, but it was fine. In seven years, I only saw a mouse once. The owner, amused by my fear of mice and rats, immediately sent the super over to fix it when I called him in a barely muted panic. Some of the expediency in averting the crisis was presumably rooted in the Airbnbs he had started to list in the building. Can't have the mice running around when you promised these random people from Poland and Oklahoma a pleasant stay in the center of Harlem.

I wonder if any of my landlord's guests saw the occasional notice from the power company demanding an outstanding bill be paid or else the electricity for the building would be turned off.

That actually happened once—naturally, right when I was in the middle of a time-sensitive deadline.

I don't know why the owner dragged his feet on paying the bills. I'm sure he said the same about me at times. My complaints aside, it was a privilege to live alone in NYC. The few friends I had overall told me that I described my place too harshly.

Perhaps, but after a while, I knew I wanted out.

I wanted my next place to be more modern and spacious. I don't need a lot, but enough to not make me feel trapped. Above all, I wanted to sleep somewhere quieter. Until that point, no matter where I lived, it was always so loud. I was exhausted with having my sleep interrupted by the screams of selfish people unhappy with the choices they'd made in their lives.

I was also equally tired of feeling as if, no matter how hard I worked, I couldn't move forward professionally or in terms of real estate.

Those middle-of-the-night tirades from DMJ and "trifling nigga" James were annoying but, rightly or wrongly, signified the problems of my life, too.

I *can* acknowledge that when she wasn't hollering in the middle of the night, DMJ wasn't always the worst person on the block to me.

One of the few times I talked to her without the need of me providing her with an entrance into the building, she talked about being a cook. I went to get the mail once, and she had her door wide open as she fried chicken and blasted Patti LaBelle. It smelled all right, but I'm not giving too much to someone destined to scream like a banshee at four a.m.

Moreover, I'm glad I didn't live on the same floor as her— smelling like fried chicken and constantly hearing complaints about a situation of her choosing.

I'm not saying that single-handedly soiled my NYC living experience, but of all the reasons I wish I had ended up choosing another apartment when I first moved, the fighting downstairs, which went on for years, ranked incredibly high on the list.

I wanted to live somewhere where there were space and walls thick enough to drown out the booze-induced belligerence I thought I had left in Texas.

That required more income, but it eventually came. After struggling harder than I ever imagined and for periods longer than envisioned, it was beginning to feel lighter.

I should have known my life was starting to change when a white boy hit on me a few weeks before the plague officially kicked off.

He lived across the street in a brand-new building built from the ground up. My building, an aging brownstone, was barely holding on with these thin walls that could not even begin to contain Drunk Millie Jackson's constant professions of living in misery with this man she says she'll leave but never does.

I was surprised that dude wanted to engage with me given how I can't help but wear the frustration and sleep deprivation on my face, but he did and was aggressive in a way I'm not used to from men in general, much less that genre of man.

He was attractive, and it had been a while, so admittedly, I was mildly curious and exchanged numbers.

My curiosity ended hours after he tried to explain the hood and what "inner-city" public school is like to me via text. He said he was teaching at a public school as part of some program for some advanced degree at Columbia.

I didn't need a lesson about either, and even if I did, he wouldn't be best suited to give one.

I tried to be gentle about swatting that away for the sake of sex, but he struck me as the pedantic type, so I decided it was best to forget I ever met him.

Some of my friends had been teasing that my growing successes meant I'd be tempted to join the league of successful gay Black men who run to white partners.

Case in point.

He was now living right there in front of me. I could get over that, but I didn't love living across the street from a building that reflected the kind of residential life I should've been leading by then.

Well, in another city, anyway.

I understand why natives are irritated by transients who pen essays or perform monologues about why they left New York City, so for the sake of brevity, I'll simply say I went there to grow as a writer and a person, and I'm grateful for the time I spent there, but I was ready to go.

I wanted something more chill and, yeah, peaceful.

But just as soon as I was ready to give notice to my landlord and vacate, I found myself stuck in my home like much of the rest of the planet, trying not to inhale death.

Not only stuck at home, but my sleep was now being drowned out by new and even louder noises.

I lived less than ten blocks from Harlem Hospital, and early on, Harlem was the epicenter of the coronavirus pandemic. When you're the global hotspot for a raging pandemic, all you hear after a while is sirens. The sounds of sirens signaled suffering and death.

For those first couple of weeks, it sounded like suffering and death on loop.

The lack of space and contact with the outside world, and the restrictions on everything most people take for granted, were disheartening, but the sounds of those sirens? Utterly depressing. How could anyone sleep through them?

Indica helped me, but not often.

It was at least nice to hear New Yorkers stop what they were doing at seven every evening to applaud and cheer on all of the service workers trying to save lives.

Still, all that death around me and the coverage on it took me to a place I hope I never have to go back to.

And when the sounds of constant sirens started to taper off, fireworks took their place.

There was almost a schedule to it for a while. On weekdays, they began around nine p.m., but on weekends, the pyrotechnics sometimes started even earlier. No matter when they started, they lasted until around four a.m.

I'm from the South, so I know bored people enjoy passing the time with fireworks. It's a year-round habit there, but this was on another level I had never experienced. June is the time of year when cheap fireworks become readily available—theoretically to mark the Fourth of July, but usually just to make a bunch of noise—but was there someplace giving away fireworks? And so early into the summer?

The sudden heightened frequency was not imagined.

A spokesperson for the National Fireworks Association confirmed in an *interview* at the time that the industry was enjoying a banner year in consumer sales.

We were living through a global pandemic and the financial crisis it spurred, along with a burgeoning race war—so understandably, people needed to find ways to channel their angst and frustrations.

Fine, but every single night for hours on end?

There was no consideration of autistic children, pets, the elderly, or the people sick in their homes.

Or for me, someone struggling to go to sleep.

It just reminded me that those fireworks are a symptom of a broader collective selfishness among so many people.

In addition to the firework shows, there were people screaming in the street during the same what-the-hell-are-y'all-even-doing-up time window. Some were arguing, but most of them were being loud for the sake of it.

I got a text from the white boy across the street complaining about the noise.

And he was trying to see if I wanted to come over—like there wasn't a plague going around and we were both strangers.

We hadn't communicated since he had irritated me.

I left it that way.

Now wasn't the time to breathe around strangers.

By then all my goodwill to my fellow humans was rapidly depleting for most of the folks in my zip code.

I did end up worrying about Drunk Millie Jackson, however.

I noticed that I hadn't seen her in a while. I saw her man, James. He knocked on my door and tried to have a full-fledged conversation with me—with no mask on.

I'm glad I knew to put a mask on once I heard that knock.

Where was DMJ to yell at this careless man?

I wondered if she was okay. I couldn't stand her waking me up through the years, but I didn't want her goofy ass to die, either. I hoped she hadn't caught COVID out somewhere, lying about leaving this man. In addition to the occasional smell of liquor on her breath, she talked like she smoked Newports and Backwoods. Those are not the kind of lungs you want fighting the virus. (In fairness, same for marijuana-seasoned ones.)

Turns out, she was fine.

After a couple of months, she resurfaced, and I heard a familiar scream as I exited my building and started walking up the block.

"Heyyyyy, Michael."

It would be a bit too generous to say I was happy to see her. I was happy that my fears of her being caught up with the coronavirus were unfounded. She still looked like Millie Jackson, but no slurs or smells of Paul Masson or Crown Peach could be detected.

I didn't even try to pretend to remember her name.

I smiled and gave her a "Hey, girl. How are you?"

She asked how I was doing, and my response was my new normal: "I'm good, for a plague."

She told me that she had been in New Jersey. I did not ask her why she was there. A week or two before she showed up, I overheard James mention to the man who owned the building next to ours that he was retiring from his city job and moving to Delaware. I kind of wondered whether she was picking up things she left behind or rekindling something with him.

I did not ask.

I hope she didn't join him. I wouldn't want them waking up folks with their bullshit in a new state.

As she'd said herself every so often through the years at maximum volume: "I'm not perfect, but a bitch deserves better."

I hope she found it, but that's her life and her choice.

I needed to be focused on my plans—like moving on to a place with thicker walls.

Part of me going to NYC and living alone was to have more calm in my life—specifically at home, where I have never felt completely comfortable.

During the pandemic, I increasingly found little reason to remain in New York, and began to question how much longer I could hold out on it being safe enough to leave.

Overall, I enjoyed the time spent in that small studio in Harlem. Even if I didn't see it at the time, I made the best out of my circumstances. And although the people in my building were not especially friendly, many of the people on the block treated me well.

In fact, during that summer and into the fall, when I was overcome with the stresses of being isolated more than normal and far away from my family, two of my neighbors functioned like play-aunties.

"You're not alone, baby. Even if you feel like it."

That kindness reminded me that the years I had spent in NYC should not be drowned out by those last couple of months. Likewise, my overall experience was more positive than negative—screams and small spaces be damned.

I am proud of what I accomplished in that apartment and am grateful for having a home and my own space in such an exciting but nonetheless exhausting city to live in.

I made the choice to leave at the end of November—right after Thanksgiving.

I never got my security deposit back.

I can't tell if that's because I left the apartment smelling like weed or the general scammy nature of NYC landlords.

But since he kept my money, I hope he put it toward the electric bill.

I knew my time in New York wasn't going to be forever, but should I ever find my way back, I can only return if I can afford the space required to avoid hearing too much of anyone else's problems.

EMPTY SYMBOLS

The day George Zimmerman was acquitted was the end of a very brief moment in which I gave America the benefit of the doubt.

Six days later, Barack Obama, the man responsible for that temporary suspension of disbelief, gave a speech that drove home for me how foolish I had been.

The president acknowledged the pain many of us felt upon hearing Zimmerman's acquittal, but ever the peddler of hope and change, he also stressed that "as difficult and challenging as this whole episode has been for a lot of people, I don't want us to lose sight that things are getting better."

I didn't believe it when he said it, but it sounds even sillier to me now, more than a decade later.

"Each successive generation seems to be making progress in changing attitudes when it comes to race. It doesn't mean we're in a post-racial society," Obama continued. "It doesn't mean that racism is eliminated. But when I talk to Malia and Sasha, and I listen to their friends and I seem [*sic*] them interact, they're better than we are—they're better than we were—on these issues. And that's true in every community that I've visited all across the country."

Obama always gave this country more than it deserved when it came to racism. But that is exactly why he became president.

To be a Black politician in the United States, you have to devote your life to lying to the white electorate.

I couldn't do it—I couldn't force myself to tell America it doesn't hate Black people.

To his credit, though, Obama has long appeared to actually believe the things he says.

I always found that cute for him, but I was taught to never ignore how racist a sizable chunk of the population is—and all the dangers that come with that. My mother was, and is, too aware to let me walk out into the world ignorant of how America treats Black people.

Even so, I hoped for a different outcome in Zimmerman's trial.

For once, I wanted to think America was capable of a smidgen of decency. I wanted to believe that this killing would not be tolerated. That somehow, Zimmerman might be seen for what he is: a murderous vigilante masquerading as a volunteer watchman.

Then the jury reminded me and anyone else in doubt exactly where we lived.

A few weeks after the verdict, I was scheduled to speak at a conference in Orlando. A middle-aged white man picked me up at the airport and took me to my hotel. On the way, he made a point to note that we were passing Sanford, Florida.

"It's unfortunate what happened out here," he said.

Yes, it was, but as he kept talking, it was immediately clear we had different ideas about why it was unfortunate. I tried to tune this chatty man off as much as possible, so I can't quite recall exactly how he said it, but he more or less tried to blame Trayvon

Martin for his murder. Something about how he shouldn't have fought back.

I'm polite in that Southern way, but not that polite.

I have a firm way of ending a conversation if need be.

I employed that skill set then and let the silence calm me down.

I don't discount the Obama presidency and its achievements, but *he campaigned for the first time like a progressive*, and by the time he left office, the limits of symbolism were too loud to ignore.

So by the time Pete Buttigieg came along, I was curious as a political observer to see how far his candidacy would go, but as a Black man and gay man, I was hopeless about what, if anything, his potential political ascension could signify.

It may not have been an artful statement by Barney Frank, who became the first openly gay Congress member when he revealed his sexuality in 1987, but he had a point when he told *The Boston Globe* that for Buttigieg, "being gay is an advantage" because it "gives people a chance to affirm their lack of prejudice."

Frank would know a little about this given his own political history.

On the *Bad Gays* podcast, a show about "evil and complicated queers in history" hosted by Huw Lemmey and Ben Miller, they chronicled Frank's political journey. How he started his political career as a trailblazer for gay political involvement in Washington, only to taint much of that legacy by shifting away from progressive politics to spend the latter years of his career prioritizing the needs of those in the financial industry.

As they explained on the show, "the 2008 crisis was intimately related to questions of race, housing, segregation, and integration, and as a gay man, he self-consciously embodied a kind of diversity that allowed these deeper structural questions to go unanswered."

These moves in turn caused Frank to "embody the transformation of the Democratic Party away from the working class and towards a suburban party preoccupied with shallow diversity rather than true racial and economic justice."

Frank is as much of a turncoat now as he is a trailblazer, but even broken clocks get it right—especially about their fellow gay white peers.

Buttigieg had his own *Bad Gays* episode, too, but in his case, has been far more up-front in his corporatist interests and the image he wanted to sell to the public for a presidential bid.

In that respect, "Mayor Pete" sought to be the white Barack Obama.

For many white voters, Obama's infamous proclamation that there is no blue or red America, but the United States of America, was the kind of message they yearned to hear—particularly from people who aren't white.

To some of the rest of us, he was promising hope as much as he was change—and it was the latter that we found more inspirational.

This is why I will always laugh when folks suggest I get into politics.

I can't feed people the kind of dreams politicians who aim to be the first or one of the first of their kind have to say in order to get elected.

And whereas I found Obama to be a great writer, gifted orator, and charismatic politician, Pete Buttigieg came across as a shoddy, boring imitator.

To me, much as he professed to have not "*set out to be the gay president*," all he did was copy and paste from the first Black one.

Very much akin to white kids on TikTok who repurpose memes or dances crafted by Black content creators.

It was funny to watch him occasionally put on the same accent Obama often put on during the campaign trail, but the more I learned about him, the more talk of his presidency proved more hypothetical than plausible—deservingly so.

The signs that Buttigieg was overdue for a reckoning with Black voters had always been there, but his champions never paid much attention until they became impossible to ignore.

On June 16th, 2019, South Bend police claimed Sergeant Ryan O'Neill was responding to reports of cars being burglarized when he shot Eric Jack Logan in the parking lot of an apartment complex. O'Neill claimed Logan threatened him with a knife, but O'Neill didn't turn on his body camera as required—leaving Black residents largely skeptical about O'Neill's side of the story.

Buttigieg was facing a crisis in his city that had been building for years—one very much of his own making.

In 2012, a then twenty-nine-year-old Buttigieg *leaped into controversy* a mere thirteen weeks into his mayorship of South Bend, Indiana, when he fired Darryl Boykins, the city's first Black police chief. Boykins was under scrutiny from federal prosecutors following allegations of improperly taping phone calls of senior white officers said to have used racist language—including about him. No action was taken against the police officers, and whatever language was used remains a mystery due to Buttigieg's refusal to release the tapes.

Buttigieg wrote that the incident "affected my relationship with the African-American community in particular for years to come" in his political memoir, *Shortest Way Home*.

It did not help that Sound Bend's police department reportedly paid out *over $1.3 million in* brutality and civil rights settlements during the first five years Buttigieg served in office. His failure to heed activists' and local officials' calls for an actual citizen's review board only worsened the problem.

Buttigieg appointed two white police chiefs following Boykins' tenure.

Derek Dieter, a retired South Bend police officer and former city council president, who is white, told the *New York Times* that year in an interview, "Over the years we have had probably twenty minority officers who left their jobs."

In a separate interview, Dieter told CNN that Buttigieg took a "passive approach" with the police department and added, "Qualified minority officers leave, because there is no avenue of advancement or promotion."

At a Justice for South Bend rally held the month of Eric Jack Logan's killing by South Bend police, Shirley Newbill, his mother, pressed Buttigieg and the city to take action on behalf of her son.

"I have been here all my life, and you have not done a damn thing about me or my son or none of these people out here," Newbill said. "It's time for you to do something."

Another told Buttigieg, "You're running for president and you want Black people to vote for you? That's not going to happen."

For all Buttigieg's list of accomplishments as mayor—the commercial *revival of their downtown* area, *the job creation* over his two terms, the demolition or repair of over a thousand decrepit houses designed to combat urban blight—they each came with an asterisk for Black folks living in South Bend.

The overall poverty rate had *declined since Buttigieg took office* but remained twice as high for Black people in the area as it did for Black people nationwide, until he left office. *According to the Eviction Lab at Princeton University*, eviction rates were among the highest in the nation. As for those plans to combat urban blight, area officials *argued that they disproportionately displaced Black residents*.

It's no wonder Buttigieg's run received *mixed reaction* at best from *Black South Bend residents*.

I never heard a resident call him racist, but cluelessness, naïveté, and a general lack of will to recognize the role racism plays in the lives of some of your residents are no less dangerous for Black people in South Bend and Black people everywhere else in America.

I deeply worried throughout the primary that Black folks would be faulted for Buttigieg's stalled campaign based on the false premise that we're so much more homophobic than others.

And *there were some that did indeed stoke* that narrative.

My work has inserted me into bubbles I otherwise would not occupy, and during his brief rise in the race, I was at a dinner for queer and trans writers when one of the three hosts turned to me and brought up with glee what Pete meant to "us."

There was no "us" in this situation.

Assuming my face began to contort before I even opened my mouth to respond to what Pete's performance in Iowa and his candidacy meant "for us," I was asked about the lack of enthusiasm from Black voters and what that suggested about his ultimate fate.

After I unrolled my scroll and read off a list of offenses, I could see the dread in their face for asking the question.

Pete came across to me as an old man in a young person's body. A gay politician who seemed more invested in assimilating than shaking up a system that has failed the community he doesn't seem to have much shared interests with besides shared space in an acronym. What was the point of cheering on another white boy born into a well-to-do family who trips his way into great success?

They tried to follow up with *RuPaul's Drag Race*, only for me to disappoint them again when I revealed that I didn't watch. I don't mean that in an annoying I'm-gay-but-not-that-kind-of-gay kind of way. I support the art and will defend the right to lip-sync for your life against any bigoted GOP-controlled legislative body and governor, but I can only enjoy it in small doses. I feel the same way about karaoke.

Their shock and horror at this revelation was palpable, but we opted not to focus on our differences any longer and turned around to entertain ourselves with other guests there.

We had nothing else to say to each other.

I can acknowledge that hearing a gay politician thank his husband after exceeding expectations in the first primary did signify some degree of change and progress.

Speaking during a special edition of *Meet the Press* from New Hampshire following his performance in the Iowa caucus, Buttigieg recounted a brief conversation with his husband, Chasten (who I actually have found more impressive in terms of how to speak about issues), that he said helped put his virtual tie in perspective.

"There's not a lot of time for reflection on the campaign. But yeah, there was a moment before we went out when Chasten pulled me in and just reminded me what this means for some kid peeking around the closet door, wondering if this country has a place for them," Buttigieg said. "I didn't set out to be the gay president, but certainly seeing what this means is really meaningful and really powerful."

How meaningful and powerful was incredibly subjective based on identity.

It might have motivated some of the new company I keep in my professional life, but I was too old, too Black, and too poor to believe I could ever suspend my better senses again.

I didn't feel like talking to that driver back in Orlando years prior, but I had plenty to say whenever Mayor Pete was brought up in work or in conversation.

I'm not sure if I made much impact, but Pete Buttigieg's failure was not due to Black homophobia; it was him following the time-honored tradition of being a white politician who ignored the Black community by and large until their ambitions called for direct contact.

It's what he deserved.

Months later, Democrats decided to ultimately nominate Joe Biden, the oldest white man in the field, for the presidency.

By summer, following the death of George Floyd at the hands of the Minneapolis Police Department, the Black Lives Matter movement was no longer in its infancy and was now *hailed* as the largest social movement in US history.

However, former president Obama no longer sounded as impressed with the youth as he once did.

On the premiere episode of *Michelle Obama: The Light Podcast*, which launched during the 2020 presidential campaign in late summer, he joined former first lady Michelle Obama to discuss social justice in the wake of George Floyd's death, their own paths toward politics and advocacy, and the importance of the younger generation becoming more politically engaged.

Michelle Obama spoke with fondness about the young people across the country who had taken to the streets to protest, but expressed lingering concerns about "too many young people who question whether voting, whether politics, is worth it."

Her husband offered an assessment as to why that may have been—but it was one that didn't completely respect the intelligence of its intended audience.

"Well, partly because they have been told— The message is sent every day that the government doesn't work," he explained.

"They take for granted all the things that a working government has done in the past. . . . In some ways, we're still living on the investment that was made by that greatest generation."

Michelle Obama went on to joke that young people know more about the cereal they are eating than what the government is doing, attributing that to "marketing budgets."

I like them, but I didn't laugh, especially as Barack Obama went on to add, "The danger for this generation is that they have become too deeply cynical in government. Not understanding that all governments are us collectively making decisions together."

Both were more optimistic than not that "folks are going to do the right thing," but once again, they put too much faith in the people who never gave them power while chiding those that did for not doing enough.

I reached a similar conclusion while watching the Netflix documentary *Becoming* and listening to my favorite first lady share rightful frustrations about the man who succeeded her husband.

"You know, the day I left the White House, it was painful to sit on that stage, and then a lot of our folks didn't vote—it was almost a slap in the face," she said to a group of Black schoolchildren in the documentary. "I understand the people who voted for [Donald] Trump. [But] the people who didn't vote at all . . . that's when you think, 'Man, people think this is a game.'"

The blaming continued: "It wasn't just in this election, but every midterm, every time Barack didn't get the Congress he needed, that was because our folks didn't show up. After all that work, they just couldn't be bothered to vote at all. That's my trauma."

I can only imagine the trauma of having to watch someone so unimpressive win largely based on the resentment of what you and your family represented, but Hillary Clinton was warned about taking the Black vote lightly. But to whom did she cater? The same folks who haven't been dependable for Democrats since 1968—after it was decided that Black people could have some rights.

The same people Mayor Pete catered to.

Other Obama administration alums displayed their lack of respect for Black folks, too.

Rahm Emanuel, his former chief of staff, went on to become mayor of Chicago—and was ultimately accused of trying to hide video of the police shooting of seventeen-year-old *Laquan Mc-Donald*. He also *closed more than fifty schools* in a single year while pushing for more gentrification.

Yet Barack Obama actually praised Emanuel after all of this.

And President Joe Biden would go on to later make him an ambassador to Japan.

Emanuel was succeeded by Lori Lightfoot, who became the first mayor of Chicago to be either a Black woman or openly gay.

I was highly critical of her on social media, and the then head of one of those historic and well-funded LGBTQ+ organizations reached out to me over it.

They were mystified that I, a gay Black man, and other double minorities looked at Lightfoot with contempt.

I explained that not everyone is impressed with representation for representation's sake.

What I will remember most about Lori Lightfoot is that when Black people took to the streets to protest police brutality, she prioritized downtown property over her community's humanity.

Another embarrassing moment of hers that comes to mind is when she put on that goofy Halloween costume that made her look like Captain COVID or something. She later made history as the first Chicago mayor in forty years to lose reelection.

I hope a similar fate happens for another Black mayor, Eric Adams of New York City, who fancies himself as some kind of "hip hop mayor."

He must mean the CEO of the parent company of some hip hop label because that man's politics scream old white Republican. He cuts public education; he cuts funding to libraries; he advocates for the *return* of stop and frisk. He may act like a club promoter in his day-to-day activities, but he's a Black mayor for white business interests.

Hip hop hooray?

Fuck no.

And while President Biden has given us the first Black vice president in Kamala Harris and the first Black Supreme Court justice in Ketanji Brown Jackson, he did not deliver on the police reform bill in his first year in office as promised, nor on voting rights legislation.

Yet all of the Black and other marginalized voter blocs will be stressed again and again throughout 2024 to reelect him because the alternative—an authoritarian racist (pick one)—will destroy what's left of America.

If you want to talk about trauma and being let down, let the record state that the hurt is not one-sided.

I no longer qualify as a "younger voter" given that I'm past the age of thirty-five, but since studies show that members of Gen Z mirror the *ideology of millennials*, I can say this: as it stands now, no matter who sits at the top, Black and brown lives are not valued as much, and our government has done little to change that.

I laughed at the post-racial America myth in my twenties.

I have been angry and saddened by both the deaths of Black women, men, and children at the hands of the State, and the rising anti-LGBTQ violence that has taken place throughout my thirties.

I am fearful for what the fourth decade of my life will look like in this country, not because there aren't people in the streets of America trying to fight back but because they have not been supported enough by the one party capable of doing so.

It doesn't make me totally hopeless, but my doubts for the future are well deserved.

One can be critical of Barack and Michelle Obama for what they said while continuing to admire who they are, what they've done, and what they're still capable of doing.

But if their aim is to continue to bring new people into the process, as they will surely do in the 2024 presidential election and beyond, they need to respect that people have very real reasons to be disenchanted with the voting process, and they go far beyond "they don't know any better."

Apathy and cynicism are not innate qualities; they're byproducts of the conditions that placed them there. Those feelings will never change if not first acknowledged and addressed.

They will not be addressed by electing more politicians who look different but talk and govern the same as what we're used to.

BETTER TO CRY NOW THAN NEVER

My waitress was kind enough to pretend not to notice, but it was impossible to miss how red and watery my eyes appeared.

I looked as if I was having a breakdown . . . and I guess I was.

She had a look of concern, but did not ask me anything besides whether I needed another minute. I told her no, I know what I want. I pulled it together, and requested what I had come for: a full-size order of the blue crab nachos and a jalapeño margarita.

I was sitting outside a Cyclone Anaya's location in Houston in the area now known as Midtown, which used to be known as just Fourth Ward before gentrification. Houston is hot and humid most times of the year, but even by regional standards, it was too damn warm for October. Yet I dared not eat inside. I did not feel like tempting fate hours after landing and checking into a hotel.

The state of Texas had allowed restaurants to operate at 75 percent capacity, which felt almost comically callous to me, a native Texan who just left New York, where so many precautions had been taken to even allow people to legally congregate with other people outside at restaurants. I had mixed feelings about eating so deep into the street, but it beat the alternative. Some local governments respond differently to massive sickness and death, though it's admittedly not always clear how concerned any of them are about whether the average citizen lives or dies based on the astronomical death count.

Texas was not going to hold my hand should I catch coronavirus and end up in the ICU, gasping for air, so I opted for the table under the shade at the right angle at that time of day.

I was already risking it by ordering dairy, to be honest. But trust me, the nachos are worth it. It's jumbo lump blue crab covered in melted cheese, black beans, and chipotle-infused roasted corn over blue corn tortilla chips. You get sour cream, pico de gallo, jalapeños, and guacamole. And because it's Texas, you immediately get offered a huge complimentary order of chips and salsa.

I don't need all of those chips, but they're there . . . and I'm going to eat them.

The nachos may be a favorite, but they don't always travel well, which is why I wanted the reunion to happen in person. It was worth it. I thought it would make me less anxious. Food had been doing wonders for me as far as mood-boosting went.

In response to the inability to keep up with all of the instability around me, I opted to try something: eating whatever the fuck I wanted as much as I wanted without guilt.

No matter how mundane that might sound to some, for me, shifting to that kind of sentiment was monumental.

In my second book, I chronicled my struggles with real economic anxiety and the myriad ways I learned to punish myself for my angst with my private student loan debt. Some of those bad habits included me occasionally forcing myself to throw up my food as a means of feeling some nominal level of control in my life. As a result, understandably, some have worried about me—particularly at a time of chaos.

It had come up in some interviews, but I explained that I didn't need folks worrying about me over that revelation. At least not anymore. It was never a regular problem for me, but it was admittedly a recurring enough practice that was damaging to my body and my mind.

I shared that part of my life after feeling confident enough in myself that it was a bad habit that I would never return to.

And I haven't.

That doesn't mean I magically departed from body dysmorphia. In New York, I would go run in the park that had way too much of a militarized police presence and use it as an excuse to get a raspberry bomboloncini from Levain Bakery on the way back. Sometimes I didn't bother finding an excuse—I simply did it.

I just knew these nachos were going to excite me, but there I was, teary-eyed and not nearly as enthused as I thought I would be.

This was my first visit anywhere since the onset of the plague, and I was there for two reasons: to see my family and friends and to vote in person.

I knew by then that my time in New York was coming to an end, but I had noticed in the previous months that year that my absentee ballots were arriving later than usual. The post office had also gotten noticeably slower in the fall. I hate myself sometimes for consuming so much news, but it made me aware that the racist clown of a president cared more about clinging to power than taming a plague—to the point where he was actively trying to sabotage the US Postal Service by way of a stooge he placed in charge of the agency.

I took that as a poor sign for the future of Black postal workers—like one of my uncles and a cousin—as it's been traditionally one of the only job positions that help Black people actually attain social mobility. That was curiously absent in a lot of the news coverage about what was going on. In addition to that, I feared that my ballot would either never arrive or come so late that it might not make it back home in time to be counted. Even if it might often seem pointless to vote for a Democrat for a presidential election held in the state of Texas, I had the means and enough contempt for Donald Trump to go in person.

I was shocked when my mom told me that even my dad planned to vote.

The only other time he voted was when Barack Obama was on the ballot.

I have never and will never judge him for that.

What a lot of people miss in their condemnation of the non-voter is that their apathy is rooted in abandonment from government and society.

But when my mom said he asked about voting by mail, it gave me a little bit of hope for Texas.

In addition to performing my civic duty in person, I wanted those nachos.

I was back home, but not under the best circumstances.

I flew down wearing medical goggles and an N95 mask covered by an additional black cloth mask. The flight alone already felt like a gamble. Right before everything happened, I saw in real time how easily viruses spread.

I can't believe I had to spray a passenger who sat by me with disinfectant. He was a non-English speaker, but I am positive that the spray served as a translator. Some people will never understand that you should cover your face when you're coughing and sneezing. This is why I may never completely abandon masks.

I wrestled with whether I was one of the selfish ones when I hopped on this plane to Texas. But I just couldn't take it anymore.

I ate well. I worked out a lot. I buried myself in work as much as possible to distract me, and when that wasn't feasible, I gave myself permission to do nothing if my spirit felt too weary about what was going on in my head, much less the world. I tried to wake up every day in a good mood with the hope that the news of the world or the sounds of the noise outside (that never ended— even late at night) wouldn't get to me.

But like so many others, I became weighed down by the gravity of it all.

The pain and suffering all around us. All that death. All those job losses and businesses closing.

So many dreams were being crushed or, at the very least, delayed indefinitely.

I fought hard against reality, but it had beaten me down.

There were only so many things I could do to evade how stuck I had felt all year.

I had to flee.

I felt ready for California, but I had my reasons for not immediately relocating. Cali's Mexican food is not Tex-Mex. And more importantly, LA is not where my mama lives.

I wanted to be home more often. I wanted to see my family more. When you're stuck somewhere you don't want to be, you have lots of time to think. I let go of the regret for being too prideful and not asking for help in getting back in years past, but what bothered me now was that I never got to show my family my life in NYC before it concluded.

I had plans to fly my mom out to NY to see my apartment and to do all of the touristy things I didn't do my entire time there—to her disappointment. I wanted to fly my oldest niece out there to see Jhené Aiko in concert. (Maybe she could get her to unblock me on Twitter?)

None of us are getting any younger, and I wanted to make the most of the time.

I didn't get to do any of those things, but I could at least come home now while trying to vote out a budding dictator.

I wanted to hear my mom's voice more in person—and enjoy crab nachos here and there in between.

I didn't go near my mom until I knew for sure I was COVID-free. A saliva test and a separate nasal swab test via drive-thru later, I felt better about being near her but not enough to prevent me from making sure I never greeted her without a mask on or got too close to her for long.

One of the first things I did when I landed back in Houston was to check into my hotel—one that was purposely near Cyclone Anaya's, which had one of my favorite menu items anywhere.

I started to get more into food writing. I wanted to broaden my scope of writing and spend less time fixating on people and their horrible viewpoints or personality traits. Because I write no matter where I am, I pitched this idea of writing about all of the spots in the city that have fed me so well through the years.

Before I landed, I realized that either some of my favorite spots were already closed or didn't feel safe enough for dining. So I decided my one and only option would be Cyclone Anaya's. But the sadness was not going to be settled with this, as I had hoped.

That's why I waited until the waitress left the food at my table before I really let the tears fly.

I literally cried into my blue crab nachos. Not just little tears, either. The ones big enough to the point that I could taste them on one of the chips.

I took a Lactaid and told myself, "Pull it together, fool."

I can't be crying in my blue crab nachos.

They are too pricey for that.

Thankfully, the Houston humidity made certain I didn't get my nachos totally soggy. I wanted to keep eating. I made good use of that guacamole and those jalapeños.

They tasted as good as I remembered, but my appetite, much like my spirit, was off. I couldn't even finish the order. Usually, I am not such a quitter. I thought to myself, *How dare I waste seafood like this.*

I wasn't even sure of why I was crying.

The crying stopped but continued at odd moments in the hours and days that followed. There were laughs and plenty of smiles—mostly through a mask—but there was this wave of sadness washing over me. I opted to stick with to-go orders for the rest of my trip.

The on-and-off tears followed me to New York and then back to Texas. They have since followed me to California.

At some point in Houston, I told my mom about them, and she raised one of the reasons I had been crying: I was worried about her dying.

For so much of my life, losing her early had been my greatest fear.

I used to worry so much about what my dad would do to her and maybe to us. Now I had to worry about a virus stealing her from me. Watching your parents grow older alone makes you worry about their mortality, but I was already losing too many people and too soon for their ages.

The year before all this happened, I lost my uncle Terry to cancer.

Shortly before that, I lost a grandmother.

I don't say this to be mean, but I felt like I suffered the latter loss fifteen years or so prior. She had been around the whole time, and we never heard much from her. I rarely ever heard about her outside of my dad blabbering in anger that we don't talk to her. As if he never played a role in that.

I do have nice memories of her.

Before we totally lost contact—around the time I was in high school, I'd say—we did go over for some holidays. There was always an odd tension in the air to me. You couldn't help but notice it even as a child—one reared in tension is already especially attuned to these kinds of settings. But she did have a softness to her voice and acted like a grandma with us.

She had an accent that I can't quite place but was pleasant to hear. She spoke a little like my dad. The same cadence, but their delivery differed. Say, if he slowed down and kept calm.

I was sad that she had passed, but why didn't we have any relationship?

I lost my maternal grandparents within six months of each other in 2007. I wish I had far more time with them than I got, but I have enough memories. I have no real ones with her.

I recognized that I was additionally bothered by how few folks I know from my large family. I hear from some of them now. They found me on Facebook, of all places. I don't mind belated greetings, but I ignore the ones that come with references to my books and the media attention they've gotten.

I don't necessarily have an issue with extra-late reunions or introductions to family members on my dad's side of the family.

I did find one cousin from that side in NYC after a couple of years.

It's been a gift, but also funny how we lived forty-five minutes or so away all of our lives but only discovered each other when we were 1,636 miles away. I try not to get sad about how long that took. Perhaps it will get better someday.

I didn't have to question my uncle Terry, though. He was one of the handful of relatives on that side that we ever heard from. I was sad that someone who I knew cared about us was gone.

It makes me angry, too, but what fuels that anger is nonetheless more underlying sadness.

I compensated the lack of familial relationships with making my friends my chosen family.

There are very few words I can formulate without bursting into tears about how sad it has been to lose a lot of them so suddenly since 2019.

I was sad about those losses, but I never had time to grieve them when a raging pandemic took over much of our lives.

I did my best to keep up my spirits.

For a while, besides eating, one of my favorite mood-boosting methods was to turn on "Balm in Gilead" by Karen Clark Sheard and smoke weed along with it. It sounds sacrilegious, but the highs I got from the sativa and the sounds of her voice calmed me in ways the meditation app I was using could not.

But highs can't cloud me from loss.

I understood that more profoundly when my friend Brian died.

When I say chosen family, it means the ability to connect and confide in people things about yourself you should be able to share with family but can't. To not make it in time to say to someone you love and care about how profoundly their impact has meant to your life is a pain I would never wish on another.

I laugh and smile when I reminisce, but the tears flow from time to time not long after.

As much as I hate to admit this, some of these tears have also been reflections on my life that sometimes teetered on self-pitying.

I don't like to be pitied by anyone, so it's even more frustrating when I'm doing it to myself. But grief can often push a person to such a place. Or me to it, at least.

The pandemic spurred a lot of idle time for people—time spent sitting around thinking about your life. I was proud of so much of it, but in surmising the totality of my life and the losses suffered in recent years, I was overcome with feelings about my past and growing fears that my future would be full of more loss.

It made me think of a comment I made to my friend Melissa Harris-Perry in a past interview for *ELLE*.

I said, "I don't do sad gay."

I don't want to talk about pathology all the time. I want to talk about pleasure and fun and joy and sex. . . . Everyone wants us to lean into the saddest parts of ourselves and our communities and tell the world how awful it is to be Black right now. I don't want people to consume our suffering. I am not tragic. I don't want to be pathology porn so I don't write it.

I wanted to be the person who could acknowledge life was hard in my writing but not be pinned into some box related to the "poor Black and gay me" trope. The trope can prove profitable, but I wanted to be a light. I'd like to think in spite of everything, I've done a fairly decent job of being one, but I do feel as if that light has been dimming.

Death and grief have had me in a headlock that I haven't successfully managed to escape.

I stand by not ever wanting to play into pathology, but my crying in the middle of one of my favorite Tex-Mex meals was the beginning of far more tear-flowing.

I've come to recognize that incident as the start of a much-needed change in me.

I have never been a good crier—at least not as an adult. And even when I did cry as a child, most of those instances were due to anger related to the most volatile and chaotic moments of my homelife. I've had plenty of good reasons to cry beyond that but didn't, but I can't compartmentalize the way I used to, which is probably why these tears started to flow and have kept going ever since.

Now, for a while there, I did wonder if something was wrong with me.

So much so that I started looking up how often most people cry.

For the record, according to a 2017 article *published by the American Psychological Association*, a study of seven thousand adults from thirty-seven different countries found that men generally report crying five to seventeen times per year compared to thirty to sixty-four times for women.

And I skimmed some Reddit threads of men discussing how often they cry. Some said only a few times a year; others said several times a month, which made them feel strange.

I've come to view crying as a healthy coping method and stop conflating the frequency with whether it makes me a sad person.

Life is so hard and can be so cruel . . . even if it is worthwhile. I haven't stopped striving every day to make each day more enjoyable than the last. I push myself to remain hopeful that the days ahead will be brighter, no matter how they might seem in the moment.

However, I needed to own my sadness, not only because I'd earned it but because of the reality that if I didn't acknowledge it more directly and deal with it accordingly, it might end up consuming me. Then I'd become the sad sack I spoke of being worried of becoming.

I'm going to smile, laugh, and do whatever it takes to keep myself going, but I can't ignore certain feelings anymore.

They're going to follow me, anyway.

So now I let it out as much as I can and as frequently as I need to.

I wish it hadn't taken so much death to embrace that better-late-than-ever mindset, but I'm making up for lost time.

I'LL GIVE YOU MY LAST

After I avoided crashing into a sea of traffic, I immediately thought about how that would have been one of the stupidest ways to die.

An earlier-than-anticipated death is already not my ideal way to vacate the planet, but I would never want to go out as goofy as going down the wrong way on a street in my own hometown and being killed in a car crash. It's partially my fault for even needing directions in the city I grew up in, but in my defense, I always drove by sight in Houston, and nothing around here looks the same.

Some things—random Black men in Jordans riding horses down the street—remain the same, but my eyes don't completely recognize the area amidst all of the changes.

The Airbnb I was staying at was listed as located in the "EaDo" area. I had no idea what it meant at the time I booked it, but apparently, thanks to realtors and new arrivals to Texas, it's a cute nickname for what they're trying to sell as East Downtown.

On arrival, I realized I was basically in Third Ward, given Emancipation Avenue was right behind me.

After all that gentrification over there, white folks are still scared to call the area by its name. If some native Houstonians were to nitpick and be more specific about these couple of blocks in this part of town, they might say I was staying in Old Chinatown. I did recognize the Kim Son restaurant my mom used to order General Tso's chicken from when she worked at an area hospital. I am obsessed with the way she pronounces it. "Tee-so" in that perfect Louisianan accent. I am a huge fan of accents. I always tell her how perfect she sounds to me when she talks. She isn't the best with compliments, but my repetition has managed to get her to accept how much I mean it whenever I say it.

I think "Tee-so" sounds better, anyway. I'm fairly certain I never pronounce it correctly, either. I don't remember the age she first brought some of their food home, but I remember just seeing this chicken in this interesting color with these tiny red things on top. I remember it being so good. Kim, who's been like family to me since we met at the end of tenth grade, still swears by the restaurant. I can't recall ever eating there myself as an adult, but I've always seen it while driving through that way. Even in the midst of a plague, the restaurant is holding on. It says a lot about the place and, admittedly, the state government, which has more or less refused to acknowledge the severity of the public health crisis spawned by COVID-19.

I noticed that when I drove by a separate restaurant in the area that kept the Sunday brunch party going—plague be damned. There were cars everywhere and more driving around for parking spaces. When I finally made it past the spot, I saw a bunch of Black folks in line and plenty more inside twerking. No one had any masks on.

I could be judgmental here and lament how life is not worth dying over the temporary thrill of throwing ass while filled with cheap champagne and chicken wings, but that sounds like a more enjoyable way to go than one wrong turn.

But even if I had been keeping still and staying in masks when around most other humans, seeing all of those people dressed for the club two seconds after noon on a Sunday felt familiar.

It's nice to see something familiar in this unfamiliar part of your ever-changing hometown—so long as you watch where you are.

I'm not being dramatic. Had it not been for very quick reflexes, I would have been the nigga that died in a rented Nissan truck. I was in the position to immediately buy a car, but I wasn't sure of much of anything besides knowing it had long been time for me to leave where I was.

The cars went so fast. I had no time to be startled. Lots of honking horns from drivers, and I'm fairly certain several people wearing face masks were cussing me out. But it was Houston, and 288 was only a few minutes away, so at least I wasn't shot at.

I suppose I understood their point of view from their side of the street, but I swore that it was the app—not me!

I'd struggled with parallel parking in the past, but I knew how one-way streets generally worked. I'm not one of those people who can't drive; the app sent me down the wrong street.

It tried to take me out early!

After the fear left my body, I had to pull over and call my mom. I was heading to go see her, but I am so glad I wasn't bopping while driving or doing some other distracting thing. I was already in Houston for a lot longer than I had anticipated. Let me not pop, lock, and drop out of life before I give Los Angeles another go.

Some of my friends and family sounded surprised when I mentioned another try at LA, but I always assumed I'd go back.

I wanted to go back sooner, but life as we understood it changed.

My 2020 plan was as follows: finish the book tour for my second essay collection, *I Don't Want to Die Poor*, and leave New York City.

It's nothing against the city. I'm sure work will take me there some of the time. I had been living in Harlem for seven years. I had a great time for a good while, but there was a lot more struggle involved than I would have liked. It wasn't the city's fault, but as alive as it can make you feel, it's an expensive place to exist. Your struggles only feel heavier there, and by the time some of those problems felt less burdensome, the time I needed to be there had passed.

I felt so tired by the end.

I wanted to be somewhere else.

Now, there was some obvious concern from those who love and care about me over going back to Houston, but I worried about the distance from my family.

I started coming home far less often because I just didn't have the money and was too proud to ask for it. And maybe I just spent money elsewhere—places less triggering. It's never felt good to feel that way, but my experiences are what they are. I love home, but it will never be as easy to be there as I would like.

I did, however, think it could become easier with effort and time.

Initially, it felt good to be home, but it was starting to get more stressful.

Being directed the wrong way into Houston traffic during rush hour was not helping with that.

Hey, Mama. I just got sent down the wrong way on a one-way street.

I'm okay. But I would have been so mad at myself for dying because I know that would be such an inconvenience to you given the week you've had.

She laughed a little bit for my sake, but she told me she detected anxiety in my voice. Her voice calms me, but I took her advice to get off the phone, watch the road, and remember to breathe.

Less than a week before all this happened, we had a greater scare with my dad.

He had suffered an injury at work that likely would have proven fatal if not for a caring coworker who knew to take him to a clinic that subsequently decided to rush him to the emergency room. That friend is also the person who had to inform us about what happened. If not for him, who knows how long my dad might have been at the hospital without his family knowing his whereabouts.

I already knew a lot of people walk around not giving a damn about other people, but something about this period still felt uglier than before. The depravity of many employers is not breaking news, but this was close to home. Even if I have a complicated relationship with my dad, I love him, and above all, he is a person.

Thankfully, the worst outcome was avoided, but I hated that he hurt himself and that we had to have that scare in an already dark year. It made my recent choice to finally flee New York and spend time at home, around my family, feel like the right one. In the first days after he got back home, anyway.

I think bumps on the head can send a person in many directions, and in his case, it sent him back to a familiar past that was volatile, angry, and chaotic for everyone else around him.

It didn't take long after that version of my father appearing that I began to question my return and whether I should stay for much longer. Pandemic or not, I need more peace in my life. The irony is never lost on me that as much as I love my dad, he's also the reason why I hadn't been home as often as many would have liked over the previous decade.

I love and appreciate my parents, but it was a difficult home to be raised in. And one parent was more responsible for that than the other. My dad's angry outbursts, often enhanced by drinking, were typically directed at my mother, but he tormented all of us with his tirades. Human beings are complicated, and in the case of my dad, I have a deep understanding of the phrase "hurt people hurt people." Hurt people should stand to get over themselves after a while.

One interesting fact about my dad is that he has managed to escape death quite a few times. My anger toward him often fueled resentment about that as a child, but as I got older and attempted to let go of that hurt, I focused more on praying for him to recognize that he is lucky to be here and to make the most of it for himself and those still around him. When I found out what happened to him, I prayed for his recovery.

It sometimes shocks people that I pray, but I do it because I think no matter how hard life can get, it's important to maintain hope—even in situations or people you sometimes find hopeless.

At the time of the accident, he was in his late sixties, but somehow cheating death once again did not make him immediately more grateful to be alive. To have his family. To have a wife who will do so much for him in spite of himself and the things he's done. To have children and a family willing to do the same.

But in the days and weeks after, watching that behavior was like being transformed into my childhood all over again.

The anger, distrust, and resentment. The drinking that takes all of it to another level. Lucky to be standing, but too bitter to see it and savor the blessing. Even if he wasn't a believer, why not be a bit happier for having good fortune?

It would have really sucked for either of us to go out early, but it didn't take me long to recognize life is not guaranteed and can be stolen in seconds. It was happening all around me. And it had been happening before the virus made its way to the States. I wondered why that wasn't his immediate reaction. Why did he take that tone with my mother and with us? And the more that behavior carried on, the more I felt triggered.

I was trying to right the wrong of such a long-standing absence but being reminded of the root cause in real time.

His anger overshadowed my childhood and followed me into my adulthood. Much as I have worked to let go of that, I don't like to be antagonized by anyone, much less him.

There was one incident where I had to remove myself from my parents' house and head back to my Airbnb before things *really* got back to the way they used to be. I don't know how else to say it: I didn't want to swing on him. If I did, I don't know what would have happened next. I would never stop unless put down. I didn't want to let my anger get the best of me. It would have been so many steps back.

I would be repeating his mistakes.

Anger, even if justified, is just not the emotion I want to give into in situations where it will do harm rather than serve any decent purpose.

I was angry at that moment, though. Angry at him for continuing to be so disrespectful, ungrateful, and miserable. Upset that he didn't get it. Yes, life is hard, but we're here. Can you not at least try to make the most of it?

I'm so glad I did not give into my anger. Later, I had to be reminded that those are his choices to make and his consequences to live with. I can only control my emotions. My leaving was my effort to go back to the calmer space I prefer my life to stay in.

I am not as good as I thought I was when it comes to learning to forgive and let go. I have been carrying the baggage of my childhood with me throughout my entire life, which has prevented me from enjoying adulthood fully. I have long said that if I don't learn to let it all go, it's going to continue to haunt me.

But I also needed to be more proactive about facing my past and triggers rather than avoiding them. I used to think distance provided relief, but in hindsight, that was foolish thinking, because there was an obvious pattern.

Since college, I have lived in Washington, DC; LA; and New York. There were some brief stops back in Houston along the way, but each stint made me recall why I left in the first place, especially a separate night when I had to be physically separated from my dad.

It's hard enough for anyone to have a successful career as a writer, much less someone like me—Black, working class, from the South, who knows none of the kinds of people doing any of the things I have imagined doing. I needed focus, and it had become abundantly evident that being too close to the root of my traumas prevented me from reaching my full potential. I love Houston so much, but it's often been hard for me to stay there longer than a couple of days as an adult.

At the same time, simply leaving never made my life any better either. It's why I liked DC until I didn't. The same for LA. And then New York. The only thing that stuck was my accent, which followed me everywhere.

In New York, the struggles were mostly related to real estate. Someone once said Texans make the best New Yorkers, but that person must have been rich. I hadn't vacated my dungeon in Harlem because I simply couldn't afford to. Then a pandemic happened.

For the greater good, I felt like it was my responsibility to buckle down and stay put. New York is a great place for people who enjoy what it provides, but without access to the stuff that makes paying such high rent feel worth it (museums, proper restaurant dining, the theater, clubs and bars, concert halls), all you have is your lonely self on an island. I was left with my own thoughts, which weighed me down more the longer I lingered with them. I was fortunate to be working throughout the pandemic, but work can only distract you from yourself for so long.

That, more than anything, is why I ended up leaving under a wave of sadness, anger, and loneliness to another place where the cycle is bound to repeat itself.

Months before I decided to leave NYC and park in Houston for a second, my mom said something that caught me off guard: "I know it's hard for you to come home, because as much as you love us, you dealt with a lot of pain here."

It broke my heart to hear her say it. I started to cry on the phone. It's not like I hadn't written or told friends as much, but I never wanted to admit that to my mom. I never wanted to hurt her feelings, because I love her so much. Many of us can have complicated relationships with our folks, but most of us dare not ever say anything that feels like a slight, especially when we know how much they have sacrificed for us.

Although she said it for the both of us, she argued that even if it didn't feel like it, it was in my best interest to come back to Houston. This time, I didn't immediately disagree. She was right to say I needed to be closer. We both knew it was time I stopped running away from the problems that were going to keep following me no matter where I laid my head. LA could wait a little bit.

Those first few weeks were generally more at ease. Some of that was because of the "easier" aspects of life in Houston versus New York, like more space, more sun, more of my favorite foods. I no longer had to go to a laundromat because my Airbnb had a washer and dryer. (The people at the L L I Laundromat on 128th and Lenox will forever be cherished by me all the same.)

Despite the perks, I was still overly emotional. I cried in conversation with my mom when we talked about what had kept me away, and I was angry when greeted by some of those very triggers directly. None of it was comfortable, but all of those emotional outbursts felt necessary.

They were confirmation that I needed to do more to overcome my past.

Much of that is no longer fighting that people are who they are, and not even a near-death experience can change that.

My dad is my dad.

He always says to me, "I'll give you my last."

He often wonders if I'm struggling more than I let on. He will say, "I'm just a poor Black man" before offering me money. He also tells me not to be too prideful.

We don't really talk about work, so I'm never even sure how he gauges these things.

Even if I don't need the money, it's one of the few genuine efforts to demonstrate affection he can do.

And really, he would give his children his last.

At this point in my life, that's not what I want from him. I want to have a talk where I express what I feel were his mistakes, and he says, "Son, you're right, and I apologize." But that's not going to happen. His brisket—the one I was driving home to get, along with a hug from my mom—is more tender than his conversation.

No one ever said sorry to him, either.

I wish someone had at least tried.

After all of the scares and the regressive behavior that followed, I started to isolate a bit. There wasn't much to do in a plague in a state where the governor gave very little incentive to avoid infection, so I made it my habit to stay clear of people worse. But that was not why I came to Houston for a while. This is not why I was spending all this money putting my life on hold. The point was to be around family and feel less anxious.

My sister knew something was off about me and advised me to get out of the house and take a walk with her. She picked me up from her Airbnb and drove us to a park to hit the trail.

I'd driven by it more times than I can count, but I hadn't actually been to Hermann Park in more than a decade. It was still hell to find parking, but the park was even prettier than I remembered. At 445 acres, it's about half the size of Central Park—another park I let slip by me after a while. Houston is known for its traffic, hot weather, and lack of zoning. It makes for interesting drives around the massive place. But there are always pockets of beauty to be found—and this plot of land used to be a nice fixture when I was a kid.

I'm fortunate to never need an app to find it.

As we walked, I told her my problems will only follow me wherever I go. She reminded me that she'd told me that several years ago.

I don't know who I would be if I didn't have my sister.

She didn't have much of a choice in taking care of her much younger brothers, but she never treated us as burdens. If anything, she protected us. I never considered her a second mother per se, but she has been something like it. And a friend.

I remember some of our neighbors with siblings in similar situations weren't as kind.

She has seen even more than I have, but manages to be more graceful and forgiving than maybe even she realizes sometimes.

She, like my mom, is one of the few people I can admit real weakness to. My sister is the strongest person I know. Being vulnerable around her has only ever made me stronger. She is the best of my family. She is also the best of humanity as far as I'm concerned.

I don't have to explain anything to her. She lived it with me. She saw it all and more before me. She also sees through me. We should all be so lucky to have someone who loves us so much that, no matter how much weight they're carrying, they'll stop everything to make sure you don't fall too hard.

Because she already understands, she is so good at centering me. We are all only here for an allotted amount of time. I wish more of us took greater time to respect that. But she helped me understand that I need to focus on what I can control. I have had a lot of good in my life in spite of so much pain. I need to stop picking at the scabs already.

I was happy to be outside in the fresh air. I needed it. I needed her more than anything at that moment. I started remembering why I was back in the first place.

At one point, my sister and I walked around the Japanese Garden. It wasn't the best time of year to see it, but the flowers were nice. I had a bad habit of not noticing much about the ground around me while on foot in New York. But part of being back here was to be still and notice shit like nice flowers. That and to give real thought to how much happier I could be if I recognized what was getting in my way. How I was getting in my own way.

I didn't want to leave Houston with a chip on my shoulder or an underlying sadness. That meant me making more of an effort. I didn't want to be so easily triggered anymore by someone else's failure to change. I didn't want to be so fixated on something I could never fix.

I also could stand to even give him grace.

I had a gun pointed in my face, and I did not magically become a new person the next day.

I did ultimately want to change my life in order to enjoy it more, but I couldn't worry about him or allow him to worry anymore.

That might prevent more moments like this with my sister.

She indirectly helped me decide to stay in Houston for a little bit longer. I still gave myself a hard exit date in light of what went down, but told myself that a little more time wouldn't hurt, and as long as I was there, I would try to have more pleasant moments with my family—and ignore my dad when I needed to.

I am closer to forty than thirty now, and I don't think it's fair to me or those who love me to still be caught up in what happened so long ago.

I want to figure it out. I want to heal. I recognize that none of that can happen if I don't start the process in the place where much of the hurt started. I want to find as much peace from past pain as possible.

I know that I can reach this place before I leave this world, and fortunately, I won't need an app to get there.

INSURRECTIONISTS HAVE ROACHES

As America had its first coup d'état, I fired off messages with a Trump supporter about the roach infestation inside his apartment.

Now that it had been decided that I would remain in Houston until I felt ready to go, I needed to find another place to stay for at least another month. I found a studio listed in the same building I had previously stayed in. I don't like change, and I knew nothing but change was ahead of me in this transition period. This was the teeny bit of consistency I needed.

I didn't have a long list of requirements. I wanted Wi-Fi, a TV to plug my Apple TV into, and, ideally, a bed that wouldn't break my back.

I know that I am now older than thirty-five, but it was way too soon to be hearing "sciatic nerve"—and even worse to feel it.

That other spot in the building was maintained by two Australians who presumably purchased their apartment solely to rent it out via Airbnb.

I respect the hustle, but not the flimsy, cheap mattress they had for the bed inside the place.

Two weeks into my stay, I had sharp pains in my back that made it difficult to function, let alone work out.

When I went to see my old doctor, he asked me a couple of questions before sending me to get an X-ray.

That's when he informed me about sciatica and its dangers.

He also used the last few minutes of my appointment to share with me the Black Lives Matter tattoo he had gotten.

You don't see that on white people every day, but I didn't come for show-and-tell.

I came for a good diagnosis and prescription.

After I got both and instructions to be careful with that bed, I opted to sleep on the couch until it was time to go.

It's my own fault for not digging enough through the comments of the listing—Black men in particular were leaving comments about how bad the bed in that spot was.

I didn't make the same mistake twice for this new listing.

Everyone seemed so happy with this spot and its accommodations.

When I walked inside, it looked like the studio I wish I had when I lived in Harlem.

It had the right amount of space to cook, work, chill, sleep, and entertain just enough people—the ones who weren't gambling with the sick air outside.

I wish I had entertained more in Harlem—even in that space. I let a lot of life get away from me because I felt embarrassed by my living conditions.

That was not my space, but it didn't matter.

The point was to try.

Based on the space alone, I assumed this would be an easy transition.

All I needed was to have a bed that wouldn't hurt my back—and the bed was quite comfy.

The decor was an acquired taste. I assumed the owner was a white guy who went to an elite school, but now that he was living in the state of Texas, decided to do a bit of Western cosplay. His *Yellowstone*-inspired aesthetic was not my taste, but again, the mattress in this spot was nice.

I'd make due.

Unfortunately, trouble came the next morning, when I spotted a roach crawling along the bed frame.

As soon as I got back to Texas, my mama handed me holy water and a stun gun.

Both make sense to me, but all I had on me at the time was a magazine. I only keep magazines now if I write something in them, but off to the trash this one had went.

Also, I am woefully vision-challenged.

I wear contacts and am nearsighted.

Everyone is a complexion to me without glasses, but I can spot a roach.

I spotted more as I went into the bathroom to put my contacts on and properly prepare for a potential battle.

Once I did, I recognized what kind of fight I might be in.

I promptly noticed there were more roaches in the bathroom.

As I started to better scan the place, I realized they were everywhere in the unit.

I had got to get the fuck out of there.

I do not mess with roaches.

When I was nine, a big-ass cockroach crawled across my neck.

I was home from school, laying down, and didn't realize that the nearby window was open.

I screamed like hell.

I am not afraid of roaches the way I am afraid of mice, but in Texas, they are sometimes about the same size.

The roaches in this place, though, were not that big.

Less scary, but it didn't make me any less fearful that perhaps roaches were crawling over me through the night.

Honestly, if it had been a single cockroach of the gargantuan size they're known for being in Texas, I'd still have been disgusted and vacated the premises, but I'd have been less judgmental of the apartment's owner.

However, tiny roaches here, there, and everywhere? What kind of secret slob are you? And what kind of person charges people to stay in a roach hotel?

I hadn't completely unpacked since I had just arrived, but for what I did unpack, I promptly put back into my luggage and zipped everything back up as fast I could. Then I stacked my stuff near the door and turned on every light imaginable.

Glad I did.

More damn roaches surfaced.

I tried to have perspective about this.

I finally felt some sense of financial stability, and it made me excited about the future. Perhaps the roaches were a sign to never forget you are always one economic implosion away from some of your biggest fears.

I abandoned the idea of finding meaning in this and shifted into anger upon realizing how hard some companies make it to get a refund.

First I had to take pictures of the roaches.

When I got on the phone the first time with a customer service rep, she asked me if I had evidence.

I guess my word was not good enough, but I found her request confounding.

Do you know how stupid I looked scanning the place for roaches to shoot?

She apologized and blabbered something about policy.

I wouldn't call it luck, but even if I scoffed at this dumb request, it didn't take long to find more roaches.

I didn't have a photo shoot, but I scored enough shots to get the apparent proof they needed.

Then came another request: I also needed to contact the owner.

In his first text, he sounded apologetic.

"I'm so sorry" and something about how he couldn't believe it. "I'll see if I can find an exterminator."

Yeah, you should definitely look into that—but let me get out of here with my money first.

It took a while.

When I called back, I was told that because the lister was in contact with an exterminator, I should be fine after it was done.

No, no, and fuck nah.

I pressed and pressed and, out of anger, hung up on the useless rep and turned my attention to the lister.

His tone shifted with me.

He had made an appointment with an exterminator, but that had nothing to do with my refund.

Then came a move best described as mighty white.

"I must say it sounds strange," he wrote via the app. "I've never had anyone make that complaint until you arrived."

I never felt closer to NeNe Leakes than I did at that moment.

One of the many ways I kept my head from exploding during the plague was revisiting *The Real Housewives of Atlanta*.

In season ten, Kim Zolciak and her daughter Brielle visited NeNe's house and claimed they found cockroaches in her bathroom—and posted a video.

NeNe said it was "prejudice."

In a since deleted tweet, Nene wrote, "@briellebiermann We don't have roaches! If you found 1, u brought it with u or it fell outta yo funky p—y! Please know I will get You all the way together when you start f—ing with me and mine!"

NeNe may never return to the show, but her spirit lives on through me, because I desperately wanted to say something similar to this goofy-ass man in my inbox.

I usually don't care what white people think one way or another, but I do reserve the right to take offense to a white man saying I brought roaches to this home.

I explained to him that that was not how roaches worked.

In order to have baby roaches all over the place, that problem had to have been going on for quite a while. He was either in denial about that or, if being generous, had a very nasty neighbor whose filthiness was now finding its way to his bottom line.

Whatever the case, I didn't bring anything to his fuck-ass apartment.

We were now speaking over the phone, and after being insulted, I lost my patience and needed to break it down.

I wish I had yelled, "WIG" or "HOOKAH" while talking to him, but I let him have it.

So much so that he gave me a fake apology and confirmed that an exterminator would be coming in a few hours.

"And you can come back after that."

This fool thought my stay would continue.

I bet he liked that I booked so many days, but, bitch, you got roaches. I'm not paying money to stay with your roaches.

I'm never going back—and I am getting my refund.

The realization that I was over this and him made him incensed, but he shut up eventually—all it took was being sent another picture of a roach.

I still hadn't gotten my money back yet, but by then I was packed and had ordered an Uber.

It was pouring rain outside, but there was no way I was staying with the roach gang.

I went back to the hotel I stayed at when I came back to vote, eat, and hug my mama and family.

I forgot the hotel structure was a lot older than it looked on the site, but the staff was incredibly polite and, after explaining my predicament, quick to accommodate.

I did remember how nice the bed was there, and since I didn't fear a family of roaches might crawl over my body while sleeping in it, I figured this would do just fine until I found another temporary living situation.

Once I checked in, I turned on MSNBC and noticed Nicolle Wallace sounded more worried about the state of democracy than usual.

Then I noticed all of the white folks losing their minds at the Capitol.

Crazy white people were on TV screaming, "Hang Mike Pence" and "Nancy! Where is Nancy?!"

They constructed gallows in front of the Capitol. Nooses were visible on the TV screen. As I continued to watch the Trump-loving mob storm inside the Capitol, I saw one of the insurrectionists holding a massive Confederate flag.

I can't say that I was surprised that a celebrity racist with an authoritarian kink went violent to stay in power—especially after openly trying to cheat throughout the election—but I did wince at the one or two wayward Black folk I saw in the crowd. Can you imagine being Black and finally acting up on the government, but on behalf of Donald Trump? We have to do something about the multiracial rise of incels.

As I watched the madness on TV, I called once more to get my refund.

Once I made it abundantly clear that I was never getting off the phone until I got my money back—nearly an hour later—I got a refund.

After that, I returned to the coverage and watched news anchors lose their minds over Donald Trump not giving a fuck about what was happening.

All I could think was how no group of Black people could ever do any of this—including just casually strolling out of the building after beating up on the police while trying to murder the vice president, the Speaker of the House, and various members of Congress.

Then I got one more message from the man with the roach motel—confirming that my monthlong stay was over and, unsurprisingly, asking me not to leave any bad comments.

Asking for a favor after alleging I brought roaches to your apartment.

Not that he deserved grace, but I didn't leave any comment.

Something told me to Google that dude's name, though.

I had a feeling about his political leanings, and sure enough, I found his Twitter timeline, and he was indeed a Trumper.

From the quick skim of his timeline, I saw posts about "freedom" and the need to get rid of the "dirty crooks in Washington."

If there's one thing you can count on from a right-winger, it's projection.

I wanted so badly to quote one of his tweets and write, "Should you be talking about dirty people right now given you're waiting on the exterminator?"

I opted not to. Not out of the goodness of my heart. I didn't want to be associated with those kinds of people.

They may not be roaches, but I get the same feeling from them.

I THOUGHT YOU COULD
ONLY MELT IN TEXAS

I was about to take a shit in a bag when I heard banging on the door.
I thought rock bottom was having to use a bucket and cold water to bathe during my final year of college, but no, this had to be it. Back then, I was renting a room from an older Howard graduate who was apparently not paying the utility bills associated with her mouse-infested home that I imagine has since been renovated by very rich people given they now dominate the area.

When that happened, I was referred to someone in housing at Howard to beg for a last-minute admittance into one of the on-campus apartments. I can beg pretty well when met with the prospect of having to once again wash my ass with a red bucket, so my pleas were heard. When I was able to move in, I immediately threw what I had back at the other place into black trash bags and jumped into the car of my friend waiting outside to take me somewhere else to live.

If I had more money at the time, I would have never been in that situation to begin with.

Here, I had more money and, for the first time, mobility on my terms, but only the very well-to-do or lucky could escape this. It's not that I'm too proud to take a shit in a bag, but I would rather that not be my only option. I'm in my thirties and deserve a working toilet. Have I not suffered enough as a millennial?

For the record, I am not a huge fan of talking about defecation. I hope everyone is regular, but I don't want to know anything about it. If we are the closest of the closest, I may mildly tolerate you talking about it because you're sick, if not close to death. Fine, tell me about your shit, but if you don't fit that description, keep it to yourself. Even if you do fit that description, try to keep it to yourself for as long as possible.

I really don't want to know.

I have so much unsolicited intel about way more people than I should thanks to the internet. Must I also know that?

Much as I hate this subject, though, I will never get over being met with the prospect of having to take a shit in a bag.

Probably because I can't say with confidence that it won't happen again if I forget to stock up on bottled water during the next storm. I guess that makes it a good thing that, no matter how much money I make in this life, I will always be one of those Black people who stocks up on plastic grocery bags—even if in some Airbnb.

Even when I laid the bag down, I kind of laughed at how pathetic the situation had gotten.

I wanted a stress-free winter, but I was about to take a shit in a bag.

There is no such thing as peace when residing in a failed state.

It had been a couple days since the electricity in Texas had been out for an overwhelming majority of us. Those who managed to keep their electricity were predominantly the wealthiest and whitest of the population. The lights of empty buildings in Downtown Houston managed to stay on, of course. The sight understandably irritated the hell out of city residents shivering in the cold. I also bet many of those lights shining brightly in Downtown Houston hovered over unhoused people sleeping outside of vacant office spaces that could easily be reimagined into affordable housing.

I understand that it is not atypical for the electricity to go out during a severe storm. Texas is not known for being a winter wonderland, and Houston's weather is historically crazy, so it is not far-fetched in theory to see why there might be problems with the power. However, the issue at hand was not that Houston can't handle snowflakes falling but what happens when monopolies boosted by the idiocy and corruption of government officials leave us fucked in this new hell from climate change.

Texas is a nation unto itself but, as Texans came to learn once the storm arrived, can't do it alone when it comes to maintaining a functional electrical grid. It is the only state in the union that refuses to join the two other grids shared by the rest of the country. I don't think I ever quite knew that fun fact until I was in the dark. I am sadly one of those Texans who love letting you know that I am from Texas, but I wouldn't want to be the only plug.

Texas Republicans knew that a day like this could come but didn't care to do anything to prepare for it.

A decade prior, there was another winter storm that caused blackouts—*recommendations were made* to make improvements to the state's grid in order for it to be able to better contend with future winter weather.

Nothing was ever done.

A lot of people in Texas are kind, but the operating themes of government under conservative rule are to be stingy and greedy while letting corporations do as they please.

It's one thing to let a public street become a pothole palace but another to subject residents to no power or water in unseasonably freezing temperatures. Texas is the place you go to melt in heat that feels like oppression. I was not ready for any of this.

I purposely came to Texas during this time to avoid winter.

I left New York at the end of November in 2020 because I did not want to endure another cold and dark winter. I had already spent the majority of the spring and summer inside a small apartment trying not to inhale death. I didn't want to continue doing that when it got dark at 4:17 p.m. or outrun a rat on the sidewalk while trying not to bust my ass on black ice. I did not want to freeze anymore.

I told myself that I was done with winter—at least the snow portions, anyway.

If there is any place in Texas where it might snow, it would be in Dallas.

The snow, spiteful and obviously stalking me, found me in Houston.

I threw out so much of my stuff when I left my place in Harlem. Much as my mom kept suggesting it, I was not going to put my name on any lease in Houston.

This lil' Airbnb arrangement—while stressful at times—gave me flexibility. Outside of a few boxes I had saved elsewhere, all I had was my two bags of luggage. I got an air fryer to eat basically salmon and chicken wings until I figured the rest of it out.

Two hours into the snow falling, the power in my building went out.

The power went out as I was cooking my chicken wings in the air fryer.

All I wanted to do that day was eat my chicken wings and watch *Basketball Wives*. That season wasn't especially great. I think too many reality stars are self-producing now.

Without chicken wings and TV beef to distract myself from everything, I grabbed peanut butter and a spoon and waited it out.

I was staying in the Texas Medical Center, so I assumed the electricity would be back on fast. I quickly reassessed the situation the next morning. I sat in the dark and the cold with everyone else for days.

I did my best to keep up with what was happening, but it was hard to follow when I didn't have much of a working phone.

I felt like one of those people from that insurance company ad about people turning into their parents, because I had not upgraded my iPhone when I needed to. I like Apple products but don't feel obligated to get every single release. But a few had gone by at this point, and since it wasn't an issue of means, I was being my mother in my refusal to get a new phone.

I don't know who put a root on my electronics the day the storm fell, but the phone I thought I had charging had not, and the battery was rapidly dropping every minute. I did not have any other chargers. I told my family in our group chat that I was alive and would check in the next morning.

Why did I not go to my parents' house? This was not a natural disaster, but generally, my dad can be on a trip during inclement weather. I didn't think to ask to go to my sister's house after the fact—but I was also still worried about passing COVID to family members. Unlike some, I took the plague serious enough to where I'd try not to infect kinfolk. That kind of funeral would suck even more.

The next time I turned on my phone, I noticed which people did and did not check on me then and in the days after.

One thing I saw expressed often on social media was this sentiment that during the pandemic, you found out who your real friends were. I found that sentiment so stupid and adorably American in its self-centeredness. I think more often than not, people were doing their best while being understandably distracted by one or many things.

That does not mean that with certain relationships, you shouldn't have expectations. I just think that in a time when so many people let us down in larger and more dangerous ways, we can stand to be more graceful if we know that people ultimately have their problems, too.

I also posted significantly less on social media, which makes a lot of people forget you were ever born.

Having said that, some people did know I was in Texas and said nothing so I did think "Fuck them, but God bless" for a few people. I don't try to be petty, but I'm not perfect, either. I certainly do not extend any graciousness to folks whom I had to remind in real time that it's incredibly difficult to work without electricity.

Everyone employed worked through remarkable circumstances in 2020 and 2021, but we shouldn't be expected to work through literally anything. I know we are largely forced to carry on as if people aren't getting sick and dropping dead all around us, but I don't have power, love. What do you want me to type, and where am I sending it?

So many sociopaths—and simpletons—are in charge of our livelihoods.

Speaking of, the next time I turned my phone on to send a signal to my kin and my people that I was okay, I did scroll through Twitter.

As vile as that app has become, it remains a valid resource for news and updates in times like these.

I only wish the useful information didn't have to stand beside so many different assholes.

This description largely applies to liberal white people—though they did have a few nonwhite friends tag themselves in—but there were people literally gloating that human beings were suffering because it was a red state? I couldn't wish ill on people at the time, as I didn't want to worsen my odds in already difficult circumstances, but I hate when I'm reminded that even human suffering is a game to some people.

After I lost a little faith in humanity, I turned to the news and read about a troll who also plays games with people's lives.

As his constituents tried to keep warm, Governor Greg Abbott spent his time doing press.

He did one local interview with Dallas-area ABC-affiliate WFAA *early into the blackout*, describing how natural gas pipelines had frozen up and prevented manufacturers from extracting and shipping it to power plants and customers. He said that while some of the state's windmills did freeze up, most of the blame lay with natural gas shortages.

But then he scored a prime-time hit later that night on Fox News and told a different story to a national audience.

"This shows how the Green New Deal would be a deadly deal for America," Abbott told Sean Hannity. He proceeded to say how solar and wind power got "shut down" and noted that those sources account for 10 percent of the state's energy—neglecting to mention the other 90 percent.

I'm wrapped up in a blanket, wanting to throw this raggedy iPhone at the wall but can't, and the governor of Texas is on TV trolling for likes.

I'm not bringing this up for the sake of punditry.

I don't have much faith in politicians generally, much less

Republicans in Texas, but I was stumbling around my Airbnb trying to get the feeling back in my feet, and this goofy piece of shit was on Fox "News."

He was so consumed with his own ambition—i.e., a future presidential bid—that as the power grid failed in his state during a storm and left millions upon millions of people without power in the cold, his main concern was to mock political policy as a means to ward off primary challengers.

He was not looking for electricians because it was more politically expedient to him at that moment to "own the libs" on cable news.

I think about this more than I should, but I find it so bizarre how people, regardless of their backgrounds and job positions, all operate under the belief that everything is content.

So often, I want to scream, "You motherfuckers are crazy!"

I read one more story, then soon after decided that I needed to be less of a news junkie.

While the governor of Texas was trolling climate change, Texas senator Ted Cruz *was at Bush Intercontinental Airport in Houston* waiting to board his flight to Cancún. There are so many wonderful people from Houston that I purposely block out that someone like Ted Cruz can also lay claim to the city. Ted Cruz is someone who let Donald Trump call his wife ugly and accuse his father of murdering JFK. But if you won't defend them, you won't bother with voters.

He did waste time offering an excuse for his actions.

"Wanting to be a good dad, I flew down with them last night and am flying back this afternoon," Cruz *claimed* to a reporter.

In addition to face-shaming Cruz's bride and pointing the murder finger at his pops, Trump branded him "Lyin' Ted."

When Cruz returned home to repair his image—i.e., *hand out a few bottles of water*—he also went on Fox News with the same mission as Abbott: to troll for favor.

As if his constituents weren't dying by then.

As if people like me weren't watching this on their phones while on the toilet without electricity and, now, running water.

Without much access to people, I spent most of the time trying to keep some semblance of a schedule.

I did my morning jig because I don't know who I would be if I wasn't bopping through the bullshit.

I didn't want to sweat too much, but I needed some physical activity and to make the most of these wipes, so I worked out with bands. I stopped that when the water gave out. I didn't need to be cold and musty.

I read the few books I had.

One of the books was written by someone I knew. I felt lonelier than I thought I would in these moments. It was literally just me and no distractions. No ability to connect with other people—mostly because I didn't upgrade a silly phone. That same indecisiveness is why I hadn't committed to a car yet. I felt stuck, and I loathe feeling stuck. The only thing worse than feeling stuck is to feel stuck and alone.

It felt good to be able to hear someone when I was alone and in the cold. I relayed the sentiment after this nightmare ended. It was acknowledged, but in a way that felt transactional.

Oh, this is so sweet. . . . Can you post it as a testimonial with a link to purchase?

I keep forgetting that anything can be content. The hustle must go on. Blah, blah, blah.

I had already been helping in that way. I was trying to get another point across.

To say that after a while, I was alone and afraid and felt a connection when I needed it.

Some of us don't make such disclosures so easily. There are a lot of pressures with being an author, so I have no ill will. So much of the work is on one person to get people to buy the book. A raging pandemic made the task all the harder, so the knee-jerk reaction was understandable given the known pressures to perform.

I'm grateful for the feeling it gave me all the same. I hope everyone buys that book.

It did give me more reason to give into my growing resistance to share—including the fact that after spending too much time cold and alone, I needed to get out of this space.

I do understand that not talking to someone in a state like this is frightening, but I didn't account for how, after day two, I didn't turn on my phone at all and let time go by without letting people know that hypothermia hadn't gotten the best of me.

I was surviving off of peanut butter sandwiches and water that I managed to ration as best I could. I was tired of that phone dropping so rapidly every second, so I let it be. And as much as it sucked to be alone, I didn't want my older parents risking themselves driving in those conditions.

And again, not kill them with a cough.

My sister has two children who take precedence over me, so I was not bothering her.

People were literally dying in these conditions, so I was more than fine by comparison.

I wouldn't turn my phone back on unless it was an absolute emergency.

I never said it, but someone said it for me.

The next morning, which by then was a Friday, I heard a bang on the door right as I laid a bag underneath the toilet seat to take a shit.

There was my mom, all five feet and two inches of herself, with her hair wrapped, holding a big flashlight, saying, "C'mon. Come home."

I asked her what she was doing here. She said she hadn't heard from me in two days and she was coming to get me. She told me to grab what I needed and come with her.

I'm a grown man, but she said it in that motherly way that demanded I not test her. She is an itty-bitty thing, but she loves to buck, and I was raised to be respectful. I didn't dare test her. The conditions I was living under weren't worth a back-and-forth. I found it too loving a demand to ignore.

I put my mask on around her and got ready. My parents had gotten their power back the previous night, but I didn't know since I wasn't in communication.

I left the bag where it was and left to go use the bathroom the way I'm used to.

A couple of hours later, I got a message saying the electricity was back on at the Airbnb and that water would be restored shortly thereafter.

My Texas nightmare was over, but some fears I had that week won't be forgotten.

In the quietest moments of that winter horror-land, it seemed like I was learning to feel the real difference between being lonely and being alone. Comfortable as I am with my own company, the solitude in those conditions scared me after a while. I wondered if this was how lonely life could really get for me and whether my aunties and friends have a point about being too handsome to be alone. Or having resting bitch face, as others cautioned.

It sounds melodramatic, but it was a bit of a traumatic experience. I wonder if a term like that has lost all meaning given the way it's abused across social media by victims of No Child Left Behind, but there is no other way to describe it. I know others suffer more dearly and more consistently, but that doesn't absolve the state that boasts of being the energy capital of the world, with one of the largest economies in the world, letting a few inches of snow shut everything down.

Not only did the state government leave us to freeze, but they either exploited our situation for professional gain or fled to another country.

As much as the state failed me, in the future, I need to be better prepared for disasters rooted both in nature and dumb men.

I had some food, but not nearly enough. I didn't have enough water. I know bottled water doesn't help the planet, but everybody knows a filter goes but so far when nothing else is functioning properly.

In the future, I will remember to always have a getaway car.

Another thing I'll do is make sure I have all of the appropriate weather-related emergency packets, along with enough water to always be able to flush the toilet when it needs a boost.

My biggest mistake was probably not going to stay with family when they were nearby.

I didn't want to be one of the people who end up being written about for fatally passing COVID-19 to their parents, so yes, I was purposely being overly cautious about inadvertently passing the corona to family members.

But part of my logic in spending time at home during these uncertain times was morbid: if I were going to die in a plague, I'd like to be near family. The same logic now applies to natural disasters and failed states. But maybe we will turn Texas another color politically by then. Whatever is less Jim Crow, less idiotic about climate change, and doesn't have a problem with Black people and speaking Spanish.

Even if I always find myself leaving them after a while to chase some dream, my family will be there for me. I am never as alone as I might feel—especially with them nearby.

So when the next disaster or civil war breaks out, and I'm close, I'll know what to do: just wear my mask and watch where I breathe.

Nature is getting its revenge via climate change and this is our new normal.

Some of us will suffer more because gerrymandering, racism, and defeatist attitudes have left their residents with corrupt government officials, but no one of us will escape.

As much as I wanted to waste battery and curse out strangers on the internet for ridiculing us, I wouldn't wish any of that on other people. I also don't have to.

We're all going to be slapped silly with storms our pollution helped create in the years to come. Unlike some of those people who piled on Texans like me at the time, I hope they are at least better prepared than many of us were at the time.

And whenever their local government fails them, I hope they don't feel taunted, trolled, and left to fend for themselves. I hope they don't feel alone.

But if it does go down that way, I at least hope they are stocked up on grocery bags.

INSERT MISCELLANEOUS COMPLAINTS HERE

Why are you looking at me like that? Did I say something wrong?"

Technically no, but the problem was how the message had been delivered.

I was back outside following years of pandemic-driven seclusion, but did not spend any of that downtime learning how to properly mask disappointment in my facial expressions. My awakened bitchy face is worse than my resting one is. I try to control it, but people will take you there.

But even if provoked, my work involves a lot of criticism, so when I'm off my computer and my phone (at least to write), I don't like correcting people. I especially don't like correcting my friends. I will let you know if you have something in your nose or teeth, but outside of that, I'd rather not.

I will divert from that stance and break out that red pen, however, if you're acting up in a way that could potentially result in my food or drink being spat in.

Here, duty called.

"Well, you were a little short and snappy with the waiter."

In my head, I meant, *You were rude as fuck.*

I'm sure my face said it for me.

I see how it might seem otherwise, but in actuality, no, I don't consider myself the Prime Minister of Politeness.

I don't have a cap stored somewhere that I pull out to defend the virtues of courtesy.

I'm even sympathetic to the irritable.

As someone always hungry but never knows what they want to eat, I understand that it can take a minute to place an order. There is nothing wrong with taking time to figure out what to eat. It takes me a minute sometimes to figure it out, too.

So, sure, go ahead and ask the waiter or waitress about the menu.

That is part of their job and your right as a customer.

But do not snap at them.

Don't speak to them in a belittling way.

That is dehumanizing.

I can't stomach that.

The waiter was already being patient enough as is.

After our order was finally taken, he asked if he should bring out the appetizer along with our entrees.

"*No.* Of course not. Can't you see how small this table is?"

She then proceeded to look at him as if he were the dumbest man alive.

And then direct her eyes to the table.

You could see the exhaustion in his face in response, along with the annoyance in mine.

Did our drinks take a minute to arrive before we ordered? Yes. The food took a while to arrive as well.

It wasn't a mystery as to why: it was fairly evident that the restaurant didn't have enough employees.

Even if outside was open, people continue to end up on the sick-and-shut-in list—years after the virus made its way around the world.

Our poor server was taking care of us and way too many sections of the restaurant. To drive this point home, I told my friend to turn around and see for herself after he left to put in our order. My friend caught herself and realized she might've come across in ways she hadn't intended to.

My friend is not a nasty person. This was anomalous. She's usually kind, funny, and the sort of friend who always likes to cheer you up. I don't know what was happening that day, but the waiter didn't do it.

Beyond my desire not to want my food seasoned with the saliva of a disdained worker, we can be better than that to each other.

Only a week before this happened, I watched a man nearly lunge at a female manager at the hotel I was staying at over being charged for the valet of his guest.

I was standing in line to check out, and I could hear him grow steadily angrier. It got to the point where I, along with another male guest, had to intervene. I hadn't seen anger like that up close in a while.

We asked if she was all right first, then turned to him to de-escalate. He was the kind of man whose attitude immediately shifts when talking to men as opposed to women. Not because I am especially menacing-looking—but by virtue of just not being a woman.

All I could say to the manager after he left was, "I'm sorry a lot of men are so horrible."

She said, "It's okay. I've dealt with worse."

I'm sure she has. I've seen similar antics from disgruntled patrons at restaurants, the airport, and practically anywhere else in which services are provided to customers.

Many Americans walk around with a false sense of entitlement. Just as many look down on service workers, whom they find to be beneath them. That air of superiority may not be articulated directly, but it is conveyed by way of their shitty treatment.

There are levels to this bad behavior, and no, being snippy at a waiter is not as great an offense as threatening violence, but asshole antics having levels doesn't make me feel better in situations like these.

I left that place wondering whether I had just tasted someone's spit.

For the record, I know that I am not as nice as I'd like to think I am.

As one of my friends, La, puts it, "You're not nice. You're polite."

I used to argue with the distinction, but eventually conceded. I can be kind. I try to be kind. There are people who can make that difficult, but as much as some humans dance on my nerves, I at least try to treat everyone with decency. It shouldn't require so much energy to be kind to people.

If you can nudge someone to remember that when they need to, please do.

⁂

I am getting a noticeable number of news alerts related to the planet suffering from irrefutable damage. How this month is hotter than any month ever—every other month, it seems. How this year set a new heating record—every new year. How much worse global warming is than scientists previously estimated.

Outside of the small bit about the reemergence of the ozone layer—which I remember as being constantly put on deathwatch when I was a child—it's majorly warnings that mirror the beginning of an apocalyptic movie.

And then there are the changes that leave you frostbitten.

I went back to Texas to avoid the East Coast winter only to find myself without power and water for days in Houston due to an unprecedented winter storm.

When I left for Los Angeles, as soon as I got on the road, I encountered flooding that paralyzed I-10, came across the stench of planet-polluting cow farts, and met bone-dry rivers spanning several states.

As for that enviable Southern California climate, it remains undefeated, but more frequently, it's giving oppressively hot summers, colder-than-it-should-be winters, and far more rain than anyone paying to live there should experience.

As for "June gloom"—that period that results in cloudy, overcast skies with cool temperatures during the late spring and early summer—in 2023, it was gloomy for the first half of the year.

The year prior had its darker-than-usual moments too frequently as well.

I returned to LA understanding that the ground moves and the entire region is a fire hazard, but darkness?

If I wanted to live in Seattle, I would move there.

And should I start hoarding bottled water?

I keep hearing about a potential drought that could threaten California and area states by some year. I can't remember—not that it matters, since scientists can't call it correctly anymore.

I'm not a doomsdayer, but should I reconsider?

I am but one person, so there's only so much I can do to fight climate change, but at what point is there going to be more urgency?

✦

Hi, Abraham. This is Aaron, how is your day going? May I give you a quote? I like the neighborhood of 1827 Somewhere Drive. Thanks.

I don't know who Abraham is, but I hope once Aaron finds him, he tells Abraham to fuck off.

I get texts like these nearly every business day from some random person trying to buy a home in the neighborhood I grew up in. Every so often, they get the name right of the person related to me. I never answer, but I have been tempted to write back, "Go away, white devil."

They are always white men. I only know this because they sometimes leave messages when I send them to voicemail. As annoying as the spam calls are, the voicemails annoy me even more.

I take a lot of pride in where I'm from—even if I know how others perceive the area.

While at the Mama Shelter hotel roof bar in Hollywood, our waitress shared that she was from "North Houston." That could mean a lot of things, but in her case, I gathered in a nice suburb right outside of town.

Correct.

Good for her.

When I told her where I was from, Hiram Clarke, she made what has since become a familiar face to me when in the company of certain types of people.

I first saw it at Howard, then in New York. Now LA wanted a turn. It matters less what the face looks like than what it says. It reminds me of the same look my friend shot at the waiter from the restaurant.

Pick your face up, sis. Don't look down on me.

There is a lot of construction going on where I grew up. It's always been an ideal area to me given its location. You can tell developers have started to share that opinion, too.

My mom says they've gotten quite a few calls themselves of folks trying to buy their home. She said it reminds her of what they did in Third Ward. And Fourth Ward. And a lot of other Black neighborhoods.

I want to give my mom the world, but I always want her to have her home.

She's not the type to give it away to them. She knows once they get in, folks like my mom are out altogether. At best, only sprinkles of colors will exist in their place—and more than likely, they'll be the type of Black person who once sneered at me for living over there before the area was "revitalized."

I think the same of them as I do of those white developers: Don't try to come to this part of the city now.

And don't say anything to me about it one way or the other.

⚬

Much as I try not to think of the state of Florida outside of Disney World or reality television, the political climate never allows it.

Years ago, there was almost a Black governor of Florida by the name of Andrew Gillum. He ran a close gubernatorial race that attracted the likes of former president Barack Obama to the state to support his bid. He fell short by a little over thirty thousand votes—a loss attributable to a number of factors. One, it's Florida, not the most hospitable environment for a Democratic candidate, much less a Black one with progressive politics. Two, in spite of the impressive campaign he ran and the national media attention it drew, it was not without controversy.

I recall him *being subjected* to an ethics inquiry after he accepted tickets to the Broadway show *Hamilton* from an undercover FBI agent, and although he maintained at the time that he was not the focus of the investigation and had done nothing wrong, that did not stop then President Trump from branding him a "stone-cold thief" in an interview with Fox.

But even after a failed bid in 2018, Gillum's campaign never ended. He turned his work to a *growing voter-registration organization*, became a fundraiser for the Democratic Party, and signed on as a pundit for CNN. His political star dimmed, but it didn't completely fade, as evidenced by him having to make public statements about not running for president and then later being *rumored to be on the short list for vice president during the* 2020 Democratic presidential primary. There also seemed to be a chance he could give another run at becoming Florida's governor.

Sadly, all of those options are gone, and he'll likely be best *remembered* for being photographed passed out on the ground near his own vomit and later being acquitted of charges that he lied to the FBI.

In the spring of 2020, he was discovered by Miami Beach police officers at the Mondrian South Beach hotel in a room with bags of crystal meth and in the company of two men—one of whom was rumored to be a male escort who overdosed on drugs, per a police report.

Gillum, who was not arrested, was too intoxicated to answer questions at the time, but he had to say more once Candace Owens, a Black mascot for white supremacy who found fame partially through the boost of another unstable conservative clown, Kanye West, somehow obtained Gillum's police report and shared it with her two million Twitter followers. Additionally, a blogger named Jacob Engels published an embarrassing photo of Gillum from the incident. In it, Gillum is seen passed out on a pillow in his own vomit, lying on soiled and stained sheets.

Stereotypes rooted in homophobia and racism quickly spread as the once almost governor became a meme.

Following that, Gillum issued a statement noting he would *voluntarily enter rehab* for what he described as "alcohol abuse" and "depression" and that he would be "stepping down from all public-facing roles for the foreseeable future."

"This has been a wake-up call for me," Gillum said in a written statement. "Since my race for governor ended, I fell into a depression that has led to alcohol abuse. I witnessed my father suffer from alcoholism and I know the damaging effects it can have when untreated. I also know that alcoholism is often a symptom of deeper struggles."

Being my father's son, I had empathy. On the other hand, when public figures do dumb shit like this, they hastily run to rehab and only invite further speculation about those "deeper struggles." And as someone who likes to tout Black politicians I feel can actually do some good, I was frustrated with his carelessness, regardless of its roots.

It seemed humiliating enough to tarnish your career over *Hamilton* tickets.

Why add this?

Following the controversy, hundreds of Black men signed *a letter in support of* Gillum.

On why they released the letter, *the authors of the open letter wrote for* TheGrio, "We did so because all too often Black men are rarely afforded opportunities to fail, perpetuated by media coverage willing to swallow us whole. . . . It is that precise reason why many people found it difficult to discuss what's happening with Gillum—we aren't exactly sure how to have this conversation."

I was less than sympathetic at the time of the letter's publication. I was too annoyed by his antics in that "We were rooting for you!" sort of way. In hindsight, perhaps I should have been more supportive given how much of a setup it all appeared to be.

According to *The Advocate*, Engles "obtained the photograph with the help of Enrique Tarrio, a [former] congressional candidate in South Florida and a member of the Proud Boys" and an eventual seditionist.

Tarrio didn't deny what he had done:

> "[Gillum] was almost elected governor of Florida. If he had won, we would have had a sitting governor involved in a meth fueled gay sex orgy with a known male prostitute as we faced down the Wuhan flu pandemic. The public would have been placed at great risk and it is likely that people could have died due to delayed response times related to Mr. Gillum's needs to enter rehab. Mr. Gillum is not a dedicated public servant as his attorney claims. If he was a dedicated public servant he would have remained dedicated to his public image. That means not cheating on his wife, procuring male prostitutes, and engaging in meth fueled sex orgies while his young children were left home fatherless. Thank God that Florida was smart enough to elect a true leader like Ron DeSantis."

If I could vomit on this statement and any pillow Tarrio lays his head on, I would.

Months later, Gillum shared that he was bisexual in a perplexing media interview on the *Tamron Hall* show that felt like an attempt to test the waters of perhaps a return to political life.

I don't believe it went as planned based on the public's reaction, and things worsened for Gillum in 2022 when he along with co-defendant Sharon Lettman-Hicks were indicted on charges of conspiracy, wire fraud, and making false statements.

I met Sharon Lettman-Hicks through her work with the National Black Justice Coalition, a national civil rights organization dedicated to the empowerment of lesbian, gay, bisexual, transgender, queer, and same-gender-loving Black people—including people living with HIV/AIDS.

I don't know anything about their case, but I found her personally to be kind when I attended an event organized by the NBJC, so I was relieved to hear that in addition to Gillum, former mayor of Tallahassee, being found not guilty of lying to the feds, jurors were deadlocked on all of the other charges against him and Sharon Lettman-Hicks in May 2023.

By then, what they had been accused of looked far less serious when compared to the antics of now governor Ron DeSantis. Say, throwing migrants on a bus or plane and sending them to another state headed by a Democratic governor with immigration views less harsh and racist than his? Gillum could have found another way to see *Hamilton*, but I'm more offended by human trafficking for the sake of boosting one's political celebrity.

And I found it unsurprising but no less striking that few seemed to note that on that same day Gillum was cleared of charges, Enrique Tarrio along with three other members of the Proud Boys were convicted for their roles in the plot to attack the US Capitol in a bid to keep Donald Trump in power following his loss in the 2020 presidential election.

The notion of karmic consequences doesn't comfort me much considering Gillum's loss and his inability to correct that loss in a future election due to scandal meant for the Black, queer, and/or trans folks in the state of Florida.

For all that's been said and reported over the years about Gillum, he was not wrong about the dangers in electing Ron DeSantis as governor of Florida.

"First of all, he's got neo-Nazis helping him out in this state," *Gillum said in a debate with DeSantis* in 2018.

"Now, I'm not calling Mr. DeSantis a racist; I'm simply saying the racists believe he's a racist," Gillum added.

It is largely forgotten that DeSantis ran an openly racist gubernatorial campaign. He felt more than comfortable *taking money from racists* and making comments about the election like *"don't monkey this up"* by choosing his opponent, the Black guy.

DeSantis lived up to his influence and has only since spread bigotry toward queer and trans people in the name of combating "wokeness."

Four years after Gillum's warning and on the verge of launching an eventually successful reelection bid, DeSantis signed Florida's "Don't Say Gay" legislation into law.

During the bill's signing, DeSantis, who always speaks with a sneering sanctimony, said, "We will continue to recognize that in the state of Florida, parents have a fundamental role in the education, healthcare, and well-being of their children. We will not move from that."

The law mandates that any classroom lessons "by school personnel or third parties on sexual orientation or gender identity may not occur in kindergarten through grade three or in a manner that is not age-appropriate or developmentally appropriate for students in accordance with state standards" and allows parents to sue school districts in order to enforce it.

Students in those grades were never taught about such subjects before this law was passed, but that was not the point. The intent was to stigmatize queer, trans, and nonbinary people in the name of garnering press. He's done an incredible job so far.

The legislation has subsequently been proposed to expand to a banning of all discussions of sexuality and gender until twelfth grade. Some of us saw that coming at the introduction of the initial legislation. We were ignored, as usual.

Already, courses related to Black history have been further gutted. As have any diversity and inclusion initiatives on public college campuses. It's taken some a bit longer than it should have to have noticed that his racism was always going to extend to homophobia, transphobia, and queer antagonism.

However, in the backdrop of all of this have been countless profiles, articles, op-eds, and news segments pushing the narrative that DeSantis is the "safer" version of Trump.

Safer for whom?

He's been touted as a smarter version of Trump, too, though that's mainly relegated to where he went to school: Yale University and Harvard Law School.

"He knows better" is a frequent phrase used in political media about his antics and bigoted positions.

There are plenty of dumb people who come from Ivy League schools. I don't think DeSantis knows better, but it doesn't matter. Regardless of "knowing better," he gets the benefit of having his antics categorized as "culture wars," which makes them easier to gloss over.

In the lead-up to the 2024 Republican presidential primary, Trump has turned on DeSantis for challenging him—branding

DeSantis a personality-deficient ingrate for daring to challenge him.

"He was dead as a dog; he was a dead politician. He would have been working perhaps for a law firm or doing something else," Trump told a small group of reporters aboard his plane en route to Iowa in the spring of 2023 for a campaign appearance.

"Remember this: if it weren't for me, Ron DeSanctimonious would right now be working probably at a law firm, or maybe a Pizza Hut, I don't know."

We shared a similar view of DeSantis's moralizing, but I liked the other option, "Meatball Ron," better, though it was reportedly deemed "too crude" by those in Trump world.

Funny, given he continues to refer to Gillum as a "crackhead."

At least he regrets his support of DeSantis.

So do I.

Perhaps Gillum would have crashed and burned as governor given his post-candidacy troubles, but when I assess the state of American politics, specifically in Florida, what does it say that a "crackhead" would have only been a better governor of Florida than its present one?

For all the bad coverage Andrew Gillum has received—admittedly, much of it his own fault—that letter released in his favor was right in that Black men are rarely afforded opportunities to fail.

In this case, that failure had a more lasting impact that continues to go unacknowledged.

I don't know what will happen in the next presidential election, but I see already that when the American press corps helps facilitate a racist game show host becoming president of the United States, they will follow with an attempt to anoint a successor made in his image, so long as he continues to hate the same groups of people.

Not all my complaints come from chyrons on cable news or depressing headlines sent to me by news apps.

This one is lighter, but I honestly mean it the most.

Black people and, specifically, Black millennials, I have a small request: please let go of "Swag Surfin'."

I'm not saying forever. I don't ask for the impossible. But must this song be played every single time at every party and event?

How about a break?

Again, I'm not asking that people stop playing it altogether. That's not realistic of me to ask. But is it too much to ask for it to be played less?

I'm hoping Fast Life Yungstaz collects royalty checks in perpetuity, but we are almost two decades later, and this song won't leave me alone.

I don't want to swag surf all of the time anymore. I did it in my twenties when the song was first released. I've done it enough in my thirties to be a good sport. I'd rather not be stuck with this throughout my forties and beyond.

Spread it out, please.

I go outside to hear *new* music.

That has proven harder than normal around select crowds.

Yes, Black college graduates, I'm looking at y'all and that same playlist that never wavers from the overplayed.

I know I'm not alone in this. I know other people who feel like me, but they are afraid to speak out. Don't be scared.

Tell your friends to swag surf at home.

Let the DJ play something else—hopefully, something new.

If that makes me a spoiler, so be it.

I can acknowledge there are worse songs to play.

Have you ever heard a song that you immediately knew would become your archnemesis?

I have always felt that way about "Return of the Mack."

I could never make it past the opening "Ooh-oh-oh-oh / Come on / Oh yeah."

My physical recoiling in response to that song has not wavered since 1996.

Some get *so* offended when you say you don't like it, but I have to stand up for the people with sense.

I fucking hate this song.

Why?

I don't have any issue with Mark Morrison himself. I even admire him a bit after learning he wrote that awful but hugely successful song while in prison.

In 2020 Morrison told a Leicester newspaper, "I grew up on the St. Marks Estate. 'Return of the Mack' was written in Welford Road prison. I'm from here."

Good for him, but if you ever want to place me in my personal hell, play this song.

I would rather swag surf directly into another ear infection than ever have to listen to it again.

It's that terrible . . . and always has been.

~

Where we can fight on musical taste, I'd like to think we can all agree that some artists shouldn't be played at all, but of course I know better. I didn't need the *Surviving R. Kelly* documentary to know that I should stop supporting a creep, but after the documentary and R. Kelly's subsequent arrest, trials, and convictions, that ought to have been enough to get the masses to see my point of view. Alas, there isn't enough shame going around anymore.

I was at a birthday celebration at a park in Brooklyn when a separate group of Black folks who looked old enough to know better started blasting "Happy People" and "Step in the Name of Love."

I wanted to step all over their Bluetooth stereo.

I had a similar feeling a year later at a restaurant in Hollywood when I heard "Snake."

When I asked the waiter if he wanted me to believe in hell with this playlist, he apologized and explained that it wasn't his phone playing.

Could you go break the phone that is playing?

After that request was denied, I then asked if he could tell his coworker that they're a horrible person.

He laughed and nodded.

I'm not sure if he really passed that message along, but at least the song was switched out.

But then I heard R. Kelly again during a trip in Houston.

This time, it was a barber who had to have been in his early twenties—not even old enough to have been a fan at the peak of R. Kelly's career.

He was playing R. Kelly's "Legs Shakin'," the album opener to his *Black Panties* album, which got a boost thanks to the #legshakinchallenge or #legshakechallenge that went viral.

Years after it was released. Years after he was arrested. By then he had been in jail for his crimes. It was no longer debatable whether R. Kelly was a monster.

He was a confirmed pedophile, yet there were a bunch of people gleefully seeking attention by dancing along to his music.

I am convinced that we don't all deserve internet access, and this is one reason why that is.

As for the barber, I tried to explain this, but with the respect he didn't deserve for playing it.

He had no issue with it, and I ultimately let it go, as he had my hairline in his full control. I left it at *You can't separate the art from the artist*—a platitude he predictably recited—*when you know directly the harm an artist has caused someone.* There are convictions, documentaries, and other long-standing evidence of what kind of man R. Kelly is.

I feel similarly about people choosing to play Tory Lanez after knowing he shot Megan Thee Stallion.

That Canadian import isn't even that talented, yet he managed to arguably grow in popularity after reports surfaced about what he had done to Meg.

If an artist has been proven to harm others and someone chooses to support them anyway, I'd rather they simply say they don't care rather than come up with some cheap reason to justify it.

⁂

I used to enjoy talking about shit like this on the internet, but I've come to be a bit reclusive on social media.

Some people in my life have noticed.

"I was just calling to see if you're okay. You haven't said anything online in a while."

By a while, she meant months.

If I ever needed confirmation that I talked too much on the internet, there it was.

There were only a few wellness check–like calls, but I'd rather people care than not. A lot of people have passed. I'll take the wellness checks as opposed to not bothering at all or not until it's too late.

The quieter digital me has since become the new norm.

I used to turn to the internet for connections. I have made many genuine friends from being online, and now that I have lost some of those people, I am grateful in ways my lingering grief makes it hard to put into words.

I can say what I enjoy less about social media overall: it's less fun for me.

It can be expensive for a writer to be too quiet on social media—the only reason I won't ever delete my socials altogether. It feels like more of a job requirement. The pressure to always be present online is usually unspoken, but depending on where I write, some editors will tap me in my email to go and post about some assignment I took on.

Additionally, I find my online experiences a lot less interesting.

My Instagram feed is now mainly a hodgepodge of men showing their butts and thighs, someone cooking, someone working out, a post from The Shade Room that I should not be looking at, clothes that advertisers want me to buy.

That's not so bad, though there are only scant sprinkles of people I actually know showing up in my feed—probably on vacation—and with less and less frequency with every update.

I have made peace with what Instagram has become and adapted to scroll through stories to catch up with those I know and care about.

At most, you will get a "proof-of-life" Story out of me every so often.

I don't want to spark concern.

I told myself to post a wee bit more frequently on main as well. *Any day now.*

I am technically on Facebook, but mainly to wish kinfolk and classmates a happy birthday and go about my way.

I owe Twitter a lot as far as helping my writing career and sharpening my voice, but even before Elon Musk bought it, I noticed the more I spent on the platform, the more it made me like people less and less.

Why are debates about ass-eating, how much someone wants to spend on a date, or anything else that boils down to personal preference on an endless loop?

I can't talk about any music artist—even ones I am a big fan of—critically without some obsessive fan and stranger ready to argue and, depending on their level of sanity, potentially dox me and my mama and/or threaten me.

My opinion on what should have been the lead single from someone's album is not worth all that. I thought to name the fan base that's deadliest here, but I know better at my age.

I'm sure everyone has their own biases about that, but to be clear, it ain't the Beyhive.

Those little bees the stans leave under the comments of a Beytheist are no match for what I see these days.

Not all parasocial relationships are crazy, but enough are.

As for politics, I can post my opinions, but with the anticipation of likely being met with racism and homophobia in response. It depends on the day how much I want to deal with that. On most days, not at all.

So many folks in media and tech have touted the apparent genius and vision of Elon Musk, but based on his handling of Twitter—including how much he paid for it—and his personal feed, he comes across as a small-minded bigot not nearly as smart as advertised.

Not to mention incredibly lame and remarkably pathetic in how desperate he covets both attention and validation.

As if becoming the richest man on Earth is not enough.

If anything, he's the perfect example of the fact that money doesn't make you smart and it can't overcompensate for corniness.

It merely gives you the means to ruin platforms and troll a company into bankruptcy.

But it's not only the socially awkward apartheid heir's shitposting that irks me about the platform.

Somehow, even after another financial crisis, the class shaming has only worsened.

Now more than ever do I understand why Bernie Sanders screams at people.

Is it something inherently American about pretending that being a few paces above the poverty line is a flex?

Then there is the noticeable number of Black men on Twitter who increasingly sound like incels. It's an issue on all social media platforms, but thanks to the right wing taking the reins of Twitter via Tesla man, it's more apparent because the algorithm has been configured to better cater to it. All because some of them spent a few dollars for a blue check, which only used to mean verification before Elon Musk ruined it.

It's a lot to block on any given day.

I'd also be remiss if I didn't mention the people who do and say anything for engagement. It is an addiction I do my best not to feed into. Not everything needs to be debated, nor am I or anyone else obligated to debate a dummy with an opinion.

I could be tweeting about the color of the sky and still find unsolicited misery in my mentions.

And much as I feel for people in pain and the struggle to find safe ways to release it, some outlets are safer than others.

Not all of it is awful, but enough of it is.

Twitter remains fine for news and following events like award shows, *Real Housewives*, and amateur porn, but an already hostile ecosystem has been magnified by a man who has all the money in the world and has squandered much of that wealth to feel cool.

I'm struggling to figure out how to get back to posting anywhere, even on some nominal level. I know I can't go back to posting at the frequency I used to. I probably shouldn't worry; Twitter, or X, if you're awful, might not even be around by the time this book is released.

The only thing more amazing than that is, even if he has wasted tens of billions to buy Twitter, other rich folks will give him more money.

People like him are allowed to fail up.

The only corner of social media that brings me any joy is TikTok.

I resisted the app into the tippy-top of 2023.

I was so hung up on the concern of its attachment to the Chinese government until I accepted that they likely have my data anyway. Would what they do with it be all that different from what some of the owners of the other social media apps have done? It's not like I don't already feel like my phone is spying on me. Whenever I say something about a product, the next time I check my timeline, there will be a bunch of ads tied around it.

After conceding everyone's bad, I finally joined the rest of the world.

A part of me is disappointed in how much I enjoy an app that does all of the thinking for me, but if you're going to stalk me in exchange for free content, do your job well.

It turns out, thanks to TikTok, I hate people a little less.

A dance to a sped-up version of Mariah Carey's "It's a Wrap" shouldn't bring me as much joy as it does, but I'm glad it has, as humanity was collectively flopping for me everywhere else on social.

There is something about folks of all backgrounds dancing like majorettes that brightens my mood. There are some genuinely funny people who seem less miserable or, at the very least, not deeply invested in spreading their misery.

I've come to see it as the right place to be online if you are dealing with grief or, I don't know, Earth right now.

I have noticed that not everything is great about it.

If you speak with a mix of ASMR and professorial tones, anything you say will be taken as fact by a segment of the population.

I wish I could give gift certificates to media literacy, but since I can't, I only profess gratitude that, as of now, my TikToks remain relegated to dances, reality TV, and food, plus the elderly and children of all backgrounds singing rap songs.

I'm fine with that.

It is my last happy-enough corner of the internet.

The attention economy has done a number on my mind. There are so many problems of varying severity that I have no control in fixing or solving. The sharing of these little nuggets of annoyance and pet peeves are how I make peace with that and keep sane, and what I do like about TikTok is that when I'm on it, I feel like I am too distracted to complain.

Whether that's right or not, I like having the option.

I hope the government doesn't take it from me.

It might make it harder to help me get through tough times and potentially tougher days ahead.

I CAN SEE MY TEETH

I never keep any of the messages, but they all start the same and are typically in caps.

"FUCK YOU. YOU GOT FUCKED-UP TEETH. . . ."

Among other insults, but the insults to my teeth always lead the way.

Normally, I find hate mail mildly amusing. I started to get angry messages from random people immediately into my writing career. It doesn't take much to generate angry messages from strangers on the internet. Be Black. Be gay. Be opinionated. Or just be alive.

At the beginning, the majority of them reeked of varying strains of racism. Over time, after I accepted my sexuality and wrote more openly about it, homophobia started to surface. Pointing out my sexuality is not the insult homophobes think it is, but some have learned to get more personal.

I can't recall when these started, but they've been going on for quite a few years now.

It's been obvious that it's the same person writing them.

To be clear, I receive far more positive messages from people on the internet than negative, and it's been that way from blogger to book author. For all the racists and homophobes who assume they can heckle me, plenty of nice people write to me. Some say I have helped them accept or navigate relationships with their queer kids. Some tell me that opening up about the other difficult subjects I have tackled in my books has helped them feel less alone.

Some—notably nice white people who I presume found me via NPR or PBS—drop notes simply to say they found my book, and while they don't get all of the references I make, they want to express how they want me to meet their grandson who owns a wine shop or coffee bar in Maine, New Hampshire, Rhode Island, and other areas that sound like they could use more diversity and inclusion.

Those kind words help, but I must admit the teeth slander stings.

I'm keenly aware of my flaws, and even if I were delusional about them, there have been other people who've expressed similar criticism in person.

As far back as day care, some kids talked about my buckteeth. That I looked like a rabbit or a chipmunk or some other animal that can bite you with their big teeth. I cussed a lot of those kids out and highlighted their own flaws.

I got braces in fourth grade. I don't remember how long I had them in. I do remember when they came off, I broke my retainer trying to open a copy of WCW's Starrcade '93 on VHS.

That is so disgusting. I knew I wasn't shit for that then. I wasn't raised to be nasty like that.

I don't think my mom ever quite got how it broke, but she let me know that she didn't have the money to replace it. The hard work of those braces wasn't totally lost—in the interim, anyway. My teeth held on pretty well until my wisdom teeth came in once I got to high school.

As I got older, I had to learn how to ignore the critics under select circumstances.

My freshman year of college, I tutored at a middle school in southeast DC.

If you don't know, middle school children have a capacity for evil that is unmatched.

I worked in a small group of tutors who traveled together to the school.

One of those times, we had to wait a bit in the car for our coordinator to show up before we left. I don't remember his name—only that I told him he talked and looked like Malcolm X, only if Malcolm X had a slight New Orleans accent. While he was doing whatever in the school, some of the students came over to talk to us.

It didn't take long for me to want to strangle one of them when, out of the blue, one of the kids cracked a joke about my teeth.

Everyone laughed.

I laughed with them to contain my real reaction. I couldn't yank that kid up and tell him everything wrong with him in under sixty seconds and make him cry.

But fuck that kid.

I doubt he is the person who has been emailing me for years about my teeth—unless he listened to us and stepped up his reading.

I have no idea who the person is, but it's been at least six years or so now. They stopped a little bit in 2020. I hadn't really thought about it until they returned the following year.

As always, they went through the info box on my site.

I'm solicited for work through it, so I'm always going to check it.

Back in all caps, I was told about my "FUCKED-UP TEETH."

I can never tell when all caps usage denotes screaming or general stupidity, but it is intentional all the same. Designed to make me feel a way. And with such dedication to their cause.

My friend Nnete once told me my teeth had "character" and genuinely meant it as a compliment.

I made a quip to her in the form of a pronouncement—that as soon as my student loans were paid off, I would put my teeth back in lockdown (i.e., braces).

She laughed and then said in earnest, "I like your teeth. Your teeth have character."

I wish I had fully embraced her words then. I would have saved myself a lot of time on needless insecurity and discovered a better method to handle deranged fan mail.

I'm not naïve about the irony. I have talked shit, so I expect people to talk shit about me.

Granted, I haven't insulted people for their looks in that way since maybe I was, like, a college freshman or sophomore with a blog, but, you know, I put it out there. I can't control how long it takes to fly back and slap me.

I am mildly curious about what I actually said or did to draw this kind of intense reaction.

I sincerely can't think of anything.

I write about divisive issues and people, but I can't think of what I've said to warrant this much attention. I don't know anyone in my real life who would have a reason to be so heated with me.

I used to reply to the emails. The responses were never long. Usually, I would just post ":)." Or: "I hope you feel better now that you've gotten that out of your system." And: "Ok."

I try to take the ain't-gon'-feed-ya, I'mma-let-ya-starve approach to folks like this.

Mariah Carey always knows best.

I mean, they can always say this stuff to my face. Good luck to that person when they do. Take that however you want.

Regardless, they have a point.

As I said, it's not the first time I've heard comments about my teeth, but my attitude then was that I look better than the goofy fucks talking to me, so what happened? My stance hasn't shifted, but I can see my teeth. I have never minded having big teeth. There are a lot of amazing people with big teeth. I refer to Julia Roberts as my sister-in-big-teeth.

However, big is one thing. Crooked is another. I know I must fix that sooner than later.

Most of my photos of me are smiling, but I did pull back in my thirties.

As insane as those emails are, sometimes they leave a sting, depending on the day.

I can see all of my flaws. I'm aware that so can the rest of you. I don't totally hate my teeth. And I take care of them, so I'm not living with total shame. But they're like a nice house that needs to fix its foundation already before the problem gets worse.

And then there's what else they signify: they look like the teeth of someone who started off right, then something shifted, and it never quite got back.

It's a metaphor for my life and how I sometimes feel about it. That I'm almost there, but not quite. That I'm one step into a different world than I grew up in, but not really. Like I'm on equal footing, but then again, not far from where I started.

It makes you wonder every so often if that is the reason I didn't get that job on camera. Or why that dude didn't work out. It can induce varying fears—for me, the biggest is always failure.

Perhaps my teeth do have a lot of character, but is it the wrong one?

These days, if you want me to grin with my teeth in all their big glory in a picture, place my nieces in it with me. Or my mama, sister, and brother. Family and some close friends can get me to smile, but I'm definitely on guard.

I don't love that quality about me.

I smile all of the time, actually, in person.

In my pursuit of making my life less hard than it needs to be, I am working on correcting this—'cause I could have a much more fucked-up mouth, really.

I have been asked if I want veneers. Absolutely not. For one, they are way too expensive Stateside. If I have to get on a plane and travel to get a discount for my mouth, it's not worth it. I'm not sure why hair is a safer risk to me. Hats?

Also, while I mean no offense to whom it applies to, why would I go out of my way to buy some big horse teeth when I already have the rabbit package naturally? So many celebrities are walking around here with big white blocks attached to their gums. That would be fiscally irresponsible.

There is a rapper with fake teeth whom I admire, but since he's accused of some horrible things, I am not naming him.

Alleged menace or not, his cosmetic surgeon is an artist. I don't have the budget for that kind of new mouth. I am going to have to get Invisalign or braces sooner rather than later, anyway.

I was told how tooth health is tied to the heart. I have smoked so much weed during the pandemic that I'm spooked at times—healthy lifestyle or not. I am a Black man; we can trip our way into an early death, and if we don't, America tries to push us there.

I will not love being, like, forty in braces (should the other options be ruled out), but if it means more confidence and help to my presumably already blackened heart: lock them up, lock them up, lock them up.

I only need the teeth I already have knocked back into place. I'd rather temporarily put metal or plastic around my teeth, straighten them out that way.

Once that's done, I can finally get a grill like a normal person from Houston.

Oh yes, I have plans.

I must stress that I like myself just fine as is, but it would be nice to correct a mistake I made in the 1990s and avenge my broken retainer.

It's certainly good to protect my heart. And to change my teeth would mean I feel like I'm comfortable enough to make the kind of financial commitment required. I want my teeth to be better and reflect that I'm better.

The insults from the internet weirdo sting, but it's my own reflection I want to feel better about.

In my last reply to this person who hates me and my mouth in its current form, I extended one last invitation to say all of this to my face.

They've yet to oblige, which is probably for the best.

I'm not the biting type, yet in some cases, it's tempting.

Until then, if you're going to write me for years about my fucked-up teeth, at least give me a referral for an orthodontist.

I'm sure once my teeth are big, bright, and white, they'll find some other shit to drag me on from fake email addresses.

I'm aware of every single flaw on my body. I am my own worst critic. And I can see my teeth.

They're not perfect. Neither am I. I still like what I see.

And they've gotten me pretty far already.

I HOPE I GET TO BECOME
A HAPPY OLD BLACK MAN

I couldn't have been more than ten or eleven—the *Ricki Lake* show was playing in the background—when I rushed to the kitchen to grab a bottle of pills.

Most of the over-the-counter drugs sat on top of the microwave or in the counter above it.

I gleaned from television and movies that if you swallow enough pills, you can die in the least amount of pain. After I grabbed them, I rushed to the bathroom and locked the door. I was angry and full of tears.

I wish I could remember what triggered all of this.

I love my dad, but in that house back then, it could have been me being tired of dealing with the spillovers of his anger from unaddressed childhood trauma.

And then there were the people at school beginning to zoom in on the fact that I was different from most of them in ways I didn't understand myself.

Whatever it was, I wanted out of it all at the time.

My younger brother started banging on the bathroom door, pleading with me not to do anything. By then I had collapsed to the floor after a lot of screaming. I got out after a while, apologized, and put the pills back where they belonged.

I wasn't really going to do it. At least I don't think so. Even if it looked painless on screen, I was too afraid of me feeling every bit of my head exploding if I swallowed all those pills.

But I did want to.

That was scary enough.

After I put the ibuprofen back, I sat down and returned to *Ricki Lake*.

I don't write much about my brother for a couple of reasons. An older brother is supposed to be protective. And overall, I'd say that's always been my instinct with him. But I failed him in moments like these.

I'll always be sorry for that, but I never spoke about it with him again.

I have not revisited this moment in this much detail since the day it happened.

I have at least broached the subject of suicide in my work.

A number of adolescent gay Black boys were killing themselves in the late aughts and 2010s.

I tried to lend a sympathetic voice to them and, hopefully, some awareness to the factors that pushed them to that decision.

I had to eventually stop.

It was the picture of Nigel Shelby floating around the internet after local news affiliates reported his death by suicide.

Nigel, in a gray hoodie with a rainbow-themed center, is smirking with a peace sign in the air. In that captured moment, he emanates confidence, humor, and light. A fifteen-year-old queer Black boy living in America looking that way is no easy feat. It takes some of us a lot later in life to find shine that way in that photo.

I so admired the bravery of Nigel in that photo in school. I couldn't do that then. I wondered how long it took for Nigel's bullies to steal that from him.

A Black female editor familiar with my writing on the subject reached out. I told her in real time that I'd take this on, but it would be the last one for a while. I try to think of work as work even if I assign some purpose or meaning to it. Work had become too rampant with Black death for me.

Much like the police stealing so many Black people from their families and communities, there are only so many varied ways you can write that we live in a cruel world and we need to both be kinder and create infrastructure to help those in need.

My pleas felt like they were going into the ether, anyway.

She understood.

I wanted to try this one last time, though.

And now I can barely tolerate the subject; it hits too close to home now.

There remain moments when I sometimes struggle with wanting to be here.

I am never going to kill myself.

Not for any reasons related to any perceived strengths and fortitudes.

I'm just too scared to ever commit the act.

Most of all, I don't want to be dead. Yet I have struggled sometimes with wanting to be alive. It's the scariest sentence that I have ever written, much less for public consumption.

I worry in advance of what attachments people will place on it.

I have been to therapy. I have used medication. I have changed my diet, picked healthier habits than sativa, and meditate, thanks to Netflix.

But life is still hard.

Much as I have come to respect that some people don't agree that life is worth living, I've tried to highlight how we don't make it easy for people to speak openly about how hard life is. Not being able to do so is what pushes them to an early exit.

⁕

I lost a friend to suicide on Thanksgiving morning in 2019.

We texted back and forth the night before. He had some things on his mind, but it wasn't a heavy dialogue. I told him that I understood how hard life could be, but that it would get better. We were supposed to talk it out and laugh that Sunday.

It's painful to accept that he made other plans.

I was in the middle of my Thanksgiving Day routine (watching old episodes of *Friends* and *A Different World* themed around the holiday) when I got the call. Tears fell, but I was otherwise paralyzed by the news. Before our text exchange, we had spoken on the phone about plans to hang out.

He sounded like himself, but simply said he had a lot going on and needed some time alone.

It's why we didn't initially hang out that weekday as originally planned. I was down in Brooklyn to speak with students at a high school that looked like it could print money. I was on a high from successfully not boring them—and earning a check—and was looking forward to seeing him.

I wish we had kept those original plans.

I didn't know at the time that he had been dealing with suicidal ideation, but it was not unfamiliar terrain for me. By then, I knew two other friends who had attempted suicide. Thankfully, they were both unsuccessful, but the reality is, if someone is determined to leave, they will find a way.

Learning of my friend's death stoked my rising fears that I won't get to grow old with as many people I care about as I would like.

I spent that Thanksgiving with the same folks who had introduced me to my late friend five years prior. Much as I love my family, I'm careful about when I decide to go home. My childhood was fraught with a lot of drunken outbursts from my father, especially around the holidays. My mother may be my greatest champion and favorite person in the world, but my sexuality was initially a source of great strife between us. Some painful memories linger, even if things have improved.

My friends, my chosen family, helped me during those times I didn't or couldn't go home.

It's hard to form new friendships as an adult, which makes the losses all the more painful to endure. That Thanksgiving, my friends and I met for drinks before walking to a restaurant in Harlem for dinner. The day was full of tears, but also lots of laughs and hugs.

This was not the first time suicide has played spoiler in my life, but I do hope it was the last.

The following Thanksgiving, I was too consumed with avoiding the ongoing plague and getting out of NYC for good to reflect on the anniversary. That week, I was packing, throwing things out, and, to curb my stress levels, smoking weed and pretending to be a rapper in the mirror. I spent Thanksgiving Day alone at a hotel in Brooklyn.

Some of my friends invited me over to grab a plate, but I ended up sitting alone in silence, eating takeout.

I was not feeling festive.

To my deepest regret, I did not get any corn bread dressing that year. My dad, who still makes the best version that I've ever had, is an amazing cook, and food has always been his best way of expressing love. That particular comfort food also reminds me of the South, where people say "dressing" and not "stuffing." Complicated past or not, I like to have as many reminders of home as possible, but especially on holidays. Still, I didn't cry about that or anything else I was missing.

At the time, I was oddly proud that I didn't let the grief consume me.

But on Thanksgiving Day in 2021, it finally caught up to me. I started my day like I always do: rolling my eyes at the news until I decide to cue my playlist and dance for at least thirty minutes. Latto gets me moving; Ariana Grande and 21 Savage get me belting (21 is a rapper, but he is crooning on "FaceTime," one of my favorite songs in the world); Beyoncé's *B'Day* album always makes me feel better.

Less than a minute into my routine, I was too distracted by my tears to continue bopping. When I sat down to figure out what was bothering me, it didn't take long. By then, I'd lost more people in my life, including a dear friend to brain cancer a few months prior. I cannot write that sentence without crying. I miss Brian. He was the first real confidant I talked to about being gay, and one of the kindest people I've ever met. I have not often been treated with kindness, so I treasure those with the kind of gentle spirit he had. I still struggle sometimes with how life can be cruel to the best it has to offer.

I don't think I'm as old as teenagers on TikTok make elder millennials like me sound, but I'm closer now to forty than thirty, and when I think about getting older, I have two goals: to become a happy old Black man and to become a happy old Black man surrounded by my friends. But too many have already been taken: by suicide, by cancer, by COVID. Much as I strive not to traffic in sadness, there is only so much loss a person can suffer without it weighing them down.

It's not like death was a foreign concept to me—I've been going to funerals since I was very young. But there's something about experiencing so much death this soon that knocks me off my axis. I may be a geriatric millennial, but I was born in 1984. I shouldn't be losing this many people already.

My response was complicated by my own unacknowledged feelings about what I was experiencing.

There's only so much working, hiking, boxing, smoking, drinking, dancing, and binge-watching you can do to distract and deflect.

Months before I moved away from NYC, my mom had warned me to deal with whatever lingering sadness and anger I had bottled in me, or else I would carry it with me into my fortics and fifties.

"I don't want that for you," she told me in the living room of my childhood home.

I'd like to think I'm not typically stubborn. But in this case, Mom was right: I was refusing to confront my feelings about all the suffering I had witnessed. I dealt with a lot of it in silence, which ultimately just made me feel more dejected and more detached from people and work. I needed to cry it out, scream it out, and not feel my pain alone when I didn't have to.

So if I felt like crying, I did. If I wanted to scream, I did that, too—maybe into a pillow. And then I continued on with the day, hoping it would be less painful than the last.

It's been a subtle but significant shift in my life.

As much as I hate to accept this, part of getting older is losing people. I'm working out my feelings about grief in real time, but I've settled on one thing: I refuse to give up on celebrating the holidays as an adult. That starts with never spending them by myself again.

So instead of sulking in my room, I spent that Thanksgiving with dré, one of my best friends and one of the people who was there for that 2019 Thanksgiving in New York. I mentioned how the loss was finally hitting me. We both understood what had happened and accepted it, but each of us acknowledged how the loss will always sting.

I might have otherwise spent that day alone, slumped in sadness. It was a good day, all things considered. André and I found solace in our shared experience. The transition to LA had not been easy for either of us. But there we were, as we wanted to be, and happier, as we hoped we would be in this city.

The following Thanksgiving, I spent it with my friend Kristian and his sister, who I sat next to at Brian's funeral. I was almost tempted to stay home and keep to myself. But I heard the voices of people I love encouraging me to be kinder to myself. To not be alone.

Now I approach the holidays accepting that they will come with celebration, but also perhaps a side of tears.

It's the best way to keep my happy-old-Black-man dreams alive.

I'm honestly not even sure of what that looks like.

I don't have many examples of what a gay Black elder looks like. I'm going to have to create my own. In my mind, I hope my knees work well enough to still dance. I hope I'm still laughing and smiling most of the time. I hope that I have lots of family—by blood and by choice—surrounding me.

TAKING MY OWN ADVICE

Some years ago, I wrote an advice column for a site geared to the LGBTQ+ audience.

By the time I was asked to fill in, I assumed the end was nigh for the site.

My experience working in digital media has given me a keen sense of when some outlets might be teetering toward the end of their run.

In this case, for all the good work the site was doing and traffic it was generating, when finance or tech-related companies buy media outlets, they often place unrealistic expectations on performance and earning potential. Or whenever they need to trim their budget, they start with the sections of the company themed around literacy.

To my slight surprise, however, my time with this column lasted a couple of minutes longer than I thought it would.

I was not sure if I was equipped to give out advice, but I considered my qualifications.

For one, I was available when asked.

Two, I know how to write letters.

Three, I'm not a terrible person.

Unsurprisingly, most of the advice people wanted from me was centered around relationships.

That's the advice most people cover no matter how they identify.

People want to be led out of loneliness and are willing to trust just about anybody to help them out.

Ahem.

I couldn't be any worse than the others out there.

Most of us are raised not to speak ill of the dead, but for example, there was Kevin Samuels.

He died of hypertension in his fifties in 2022. At the time of his death, Samuels was with a mystery woman and collapsed in his apartment. Samuels used to make proclamations such as *single women who are thirty-five years old* and over are "leftover women."

He routinely bashed women for not living up to his standard; his death revealed he couldn't match it himself. But people like this can capitalize on the fear of not attaining a relationship or relationship status by a specific age.

Before the site fell into the internet ether (before being resurrected sometime later), I found out after the fact that one of my advice columns was the most trafficked for the site that year.

I'm not a braggart, but that's no easy feat on a site themed a lot around sex, with much more appealing imagery than my words on a screen.

The headline did it all: "I'm 40 and Have Never Had a Relationship. Is It Too Late?"

Writing anonymously, the person wrote:

I am 40 and have never had a long-term relationship before, even though I have been out since I have been 20 years old.

I've hooked up on numerous occasions but have never really found the right person for me. Whenever I have managed to grow close to someone, they have either backed away or I have ended it.

Nearly all my friends are in long-term relationships, and I am the last one. I am in awe of how people do it as I have never been able to.

I worry that I will never ever find someone, and now that I am 40 I am over the hill and will never have the relationship I have longed for.'

Any advice would be greatly appreciated.

—Anon

I was barely into my thirties, but I am a late bloomer myself, so I did as best I could in my response:

You sound like my biggest fear. I say that with no sense of joy or any intent to mock or belittle. But yes, this letter is my biggest fear, and frankly, it is probably one of the greatest fears for many of the people reading our exchange at this very moment. It's one thing to be comfortable being alone, another to feel lonely. It's even more painful to feel as though you will stay lonely. It's a certain kind of hope that you should never really let go of.

Mere hours before writing a response to you, a dear friend of mine, a straight woman, mentioned not feeling her best. When I asked why, she said it was because she was dying alone. I failed her a bit in that moment, but I don't want to fail you now.

As gay men, the reality is we are the first among us to truly have the opportunity to even form the sort of relationships you're longing for. I could go on and on about the perils of living up to heteronormativity, but you don't want to hear that right now and I don't blame you because I don't want to be alone forever either, bitch.

Still, it must be said: give yourself a break.

You are one of the first of your kind to live out loud and it's not as if you were given an instruction guide on how to find love and keep it. You are becoming the instructional guide. As am I. It sucks, but what can we do but live in the world as it is not how we wished it to be.

You may have made some mistakes in the past, but forgive yourself for that and move on. I know that sounds easier said than done, but you're carrying baggage with you and that load isn't going to get you to where you want to be any sooner.

I'm sorry that you are the sole member of your friend group without a long-term relationship. You don't have to stay that way, though. How proactive are you being about it? Where do you go to meet men? Are you asking for help? Are you broadening the pool of men you are open to dating?

Are you dating younger? Older? Have you tried online dating outside of the apps? The answer to all of these questions can be yes, but my answer would be the same: keep trying anyway. I know how exhausting and overwhelming it can all feel, but we have to keep trying. And if you tell yourself that you will not die alone, you will not. Because you will keep trying. Because it is all you can do. I'm going to go back and tell my friend the same thing.

You are not over the hill. You are not doomed to a lonely life. It's just been harder for you than it has been for others, but later is not the same as never. Hold on to that.

I suppose I could have provided a link for sex toys given the outlet I was writing this for, but I didn't want to assume.

I don't know what came of the person who wrote this, but I hope they are feeling less lonely now than they did at the time.

If I could go back and retool my answer, I would add that I wouldn't be surprised if at least some of those friends referenced were in open relationships.

In some ways, I love that queer people feel the freedom to chase after the goals of straight people, but for the most part, I wish we wouldn't run races not originally designed with us in mind.

I remind myself now that the headline of the letter and its content hit closer to home.

I am right at the edge of turning forty and in the exact same position.

I don't think being single is the worst thing in the world, but there have been moments since 2020 where rushes of loneliness filled me.

When the sirens and fireworks were so loud in the spring and summer of 2020 that I could barely sleep. When water and electricity were off during a winter storm in the state of Texas and I lost the feeling in my toes the year after. Losing the feeling in your toes can spawn a lot of regret.

As will the untimely deaths of many of your friends.

I wish I could be like Tim Gunn sometimes. He once gave an interview on an ABC show called *The Revolution* where he revealed he hadn't had sex in nearly thirty years.

"Do I feel like less of a person for it? No!" he explained. "I am a perfectly happy, fulfilled individual."

Gunn said he self-imposed celibacy *as* AIDS began ravaging the gay community—a fear that once haunted me and gave me my own issues with intimacy. Gunn said he had no regrets. "I am happy to be healthy and alive, quite frankly."

I admire that kind of discipline. My past issues have instilled in me the capacity for restraint, but life is short, and sex is great. I genuinely envy the level of contentment he can find in celibacy because I know I would explode after a while.

I did at least manage to go without sex at the start of the pandemic.

A semi routine person hit me up in the first few months, trying to come over—insisting it would be fine.

I didn't want to risk inhaling death.

I never saw him again.

By the time I got to Texas, I had a change of heart.

I wasn't vaccinated near the end of 2020, but I googled things like "Can you get head with a mask on and not die?"

Without a concrete answer, I opted to eventually take the risk and stay away from other people until I got a negative test result afterward. I regret nothing. I held out as long as I could. I'm no Tim Gunn.

I probably could have had a relationship already if I wanted one. My friends confirmed as much.

While at a party, one of them said, *"Michael pulls, but he just don't want nobody."*

This is the same friend who informed me that someone referred to me as a "cute curmudgeon." I disagree with the noun, but at least the adjective attached is nice.

Some of the people I used to date or have "situationships" with reached out to me throughout the pandemic. One in particular wanted to apologize and reconnect in a way that did not seem to make sense for either one of us. I said as much in my response.

Another ghost appeared months later with a different approach for a similar goal.

There's only one person I wish I could be with, no matter how much time has passed by.

I have felt it since the moment we spoke and felt it more strongly when I first laid eyes on him. I said I would never write about him, so I won't go any further than saying never say never, but I don't believe that friendship will ever blossom into what I want it to be.

I don't like it. It hurts to even think about it, much less write it for consumption. But I can accept it.

My only hope is that this vague admission doesn't count as a broken promise.

I know that I have taken my sweet time in relationships, and I recognize that I'm not getting any younger, but I prefer peace before partnership. In that pursuit, I have worked to let go of what I thought my life would be and chosen instead to make the most of life regardless of my dating status.

To me, being more at peace with myself would only make me a better person and partner.

I try to stress this to some of my friends struggling to find someone and get on with their lives. To marry and have children. Some are trying to catch up with their other friends.

No matter if you're queer, straight, or whatever in between, loneliness is terrifying.

We're all conditioned to believe loneliness becomes an inescapable consequence of squandering too much time.

That was the fear emanating in that letter.

It's a fear more of us are facing as we enter middle age.

The first date I went on once it felt safe enough to be outside was with someone who wanted to know if I planned to have children.

This subject has come up in conversation with many of the gay Black men I have met over the years, so I wasn't surprised. All I said was I'm no longer sure, but it would be nice. Nice in theory, anyway.

He was younger, which slightly intimidated me.

I have since noticed that there is a slight benefit, in that many of them only a few years younger than me don't carry some of the same burdens men older—or even my age—have. They act freer.

We should all be so lucky, though I question whether in this increasingly hostile environment to queer and trans people if that pattern will continue.

It had been a long time since I had been out and thought, *Michael, shut the fuck up. You're talking too much.*

I missed being this anxious. I only get anxious when I care to impress. I don't often care enough about what others think of me in that way to normally aim to impress. I interpreted the next morning as a good sign.

Unfortunately, he told me he had only recently got out of a relationship—indirectly, initially. He mentioned "my ex" more than once. I asked about the ex for a second. After I did, I assumed they would get back together. They did a few weeks later.

Good for them; it's fine that it didn't work out.

What matters is that I got to smile, I got to flirt, and I was able to remind myself of what all this felt like.

And, of course, I'll be around if they break up.

The greater purpose is to put myself back out there. To try new things. Maybe I'll get a different result.

Another new thing for me was going on an actual date with a white dude.

My romantic and sexual experiences with white men are inherently limited.

Then, near the end of my run in NYC, I let some white boy give me head in a bathroom.

When he unzipped for reciprocation, I shook my head, laughed in his face, and went back to the bar.

I've already acknowledged that I find most dicks ugly, and giving head in return is an option only available to a small few.

Thank you for your service, but get that pink thing away from me.

Going on an actual date felt different.

It wasn't the spirit of Tamera that got the best of me.

(To save the uninformed from putting this down and going to Urban Dictionary, it's a joke made about a certain famous twin sister and interracial dating.)

I wasn't in pursuit of finding out what all the fuss had been about.

We matched on Tinder, an app I hadn't used in years to go on a date with anyone.

It's very vintage of me, but I like to go out and meet people.

If I'm being contemporary, I just DM people on Instagram.

But it had been at least two years since I was actively outside. I had to revisit how to meet people.

Surprisingly, when I asked my friend dré about whether I should really go on this date, he encouraged me. However, I could still hear the warning my friend Angela randomly gave me a few months before: "Michael, please don't end up with a white man." She said it out of the blue while we were walking. I asked her if she felt a lot more money was about to come find me or something.

Or maybe it was just her knowing I was moving to LA, where, depending on the location, it's not always the easiest to find Black couples.

I didn't share any of that with the date, but I did note it was a first for me.

Technically, this is not a big deal. Everyone can date whomever they want, and dating outside of your race doesn't necessarily say anything about one's relationship to their race or ethnicity. At the same time, I don't plan to end up in an online thread of Black men who end up with white partners.

It took several months after we matched for me to go on the date itself.

In all honesty, I lost the energy to date some months into my LA move, after a friend of mine died.

We were supposed to initially go out around the same time I traveled for the funeral.

I didn't have the energy to date anymore. I was too busy being too sad about too many unexpected losses. When I did bother to go out, I only wanted to be around what felt familiar and what made me feel good.

I told him this at the time, but every so often over those months, he reached out and asked how I was doing. He was very kind and incredibly patient with me after I kept canceling on him. He was kind in a way that I had to come to recognize was not all that common—at least in my experience.

Eventually I told myself, out of courtesy alone, I should at least try.

Once I met him in person, his kindness proved not to be an act. He was admittedly nice to look at, but we were not a match.

After the first date, we continued to text, and that's when I recognized that though he may have been attractive, smart, and funny, we lived on different planets.

I'll concede that it can be hard to decipher context in text, but on the other hand, if I have to explain a joke in detail over text because it triggered your white guilt, let me save us the trouble now.

I have to do too much explaining in my professional life as is.

I want a break from that in my personal life.

Maybe there's a gay Chet Hanks out there who might have been a better fit, but I let that situation promptly die and returned to the awkwardness from my usual dating pool.

Like the sort of date I went on with the guy who wanted a partner who checked all of his boxes. I felt like a contestant on a dating show. I could have been any person on the planet, and I doubt it would have mattered so long as I looked good in whatever pictures he planned to post in the future.

I couldn't wait to get out of there and go home.

That managed to still be better than the date I went on with the anti-vaxxer.

I try to avoid conversations with those types of people at all costs.

When I was getting a photo at a CVS to renew my passport, the girl who took my picture asked me if I was getting the COVID vaccine. She then warned me that her mother, a pastor, had told her that it was a microchip.

He didn't sound as silly as she did, but close enough.

Serves me right for briefly forgetting that people with degrees are as prone to conspiracy and contrarian viewpoints as anyone else. In spite of my contempt for the you-should-do-your-research demo, the restaurant he picked was nice.

And you know what? When I find the right date, I'll have to take him there sometime.

HOW IT FEEL OUTSIDE?

Many find the topic to be banal, but I actually don't mind talking about the weather.

I don't love small talk, yet the weather is the safest entry point we have into a conversation with some people.

Kind of how, more often than not, whenever I contact a person via text or email, I offer some version of hello and ask, "How are you?"

I always ask it in earnest; some folks find that question fake no matter who asks it. Fair enough, though I ask it for no other reason than you never know what a person is going through at a given moment. I would rather ask the question before I get into whatever else I want to talk about. The person can choose to answer however they feel.

Sometimes it's hard to even ask my dad that question. I never know how he might respond. That makes me unsure if I want to really know, even if I have the habit of asking.

This is exactly why I don't mind talking about the weather—or at least beginning with a discussion of it.

Much as we might love a person, it's not necessarily easy to hold on to a conversation with them.

In some cases, so much has happened, yet so much has been left unsaid about any of it, that you never know where to start talking now. Or maybe you honestly never knew where to begin, and this has long been the best either of you could come up with to fill the space.

When your relationship is familial but barely functional, the weather is perfect because of its banality, not in spite of it.

This is the case with my dad and me on the phone. We only speak but so much in person, so it requires even more effort over the phone. I'm not physically around a lot of the time, but I don't want to ghost my dad.

In recent years, some folks—friends, acquaintances, or people who have read or interviewed me about some of my books—have told me that they are surprised that, in spite of what I have written about my father, I maintain some regular-enough contact with him.

It's as if they've never met Black people or, rather, people.

But yes, I do talk to my dad.

Every couple of weeks or so.

I talk to him about the weather 'cause it's often the easiest starting point for us.

If I ever felt that it was not in my best interest to speak with him, I would do what was necessary. I try to never allow it to reach that point. We're both too old now.

None of that means we ever have a lot to say to each other.

The calls last only a few minutes at maximum, but more often than not, are only about a minute long. If he calls first, he will ask what it's like outside where I am.

After that, he might say something about his job.

In his last years he worked, there was growing frustration with the way he had been treated.

He had every right to be upset.

There is always a high volume of profanity happening, no matter the mood.

He is the root cause for my frequent use of profanity that began when I was a kid. He also talks at the speed of a tornado. I get that from him, too.

I don't talk about my work with my dad. He's never asked about it. I'm not sure if that's for better or for worse, but ultimately, I don't think it matters all that much.

Besides, I don't feel right complaining about work to someone who spent decades giving their physical body to a job.

The alternatives feel better.

Yeah, Pop, it's cold as fuck in Harlem.

Nah, Pop, it's surprisingly warm now.

Yeah, Pop, it's nice out in LA.

More easier to navigate than comments like "I'm struggling with this essay about how you make it so hard to love you sometimes."

There are times when he calls standing by some friend of his I don't always remember.

"MIKE, YOU REMEMBER JOHNNY?!"

Johnny, a nigga I do not recall, hops on the phone and talks about knowing me since I was four years old. They often sound like happy, drunk musings. I'm glad my dad has people to talk to. He occasionally continues to complain about not being able to talk to us. He complains a lot. Probably why some of those friends come and go.

I always hope the person on the phone—whoever the hell it is—leaves on a good note. You never know with that slick mouth of his.

Other times he will talk about football. I don't know as much about sports as someone who still dares to dream of being the spouse of a professional athlete (ideally the NBA), but I do know that the Houston Texans never fail to disappoint my parents.

We can fill up the few minutes we talk on the phone more easily if we focus on food.

No one is bringing up deer sausage to me. Or fried rabbit. Not with that amount of passion, anyway.

He has clung to a compliment I gave his turkey wings. For all of the Slap Ya Mama seasoning I use, I can't quite capture the way he makes it. It could be based on how he primarily cooks them outside on a BBQ pit and not in an oven.

With my dad, who, for the record, now looks like Katt Williams entering his peak AARP period, that's specifically all the food he makes for me that he knows I cannot experience anywhere else but home.

On those every-so-often calls, he usually makes it a point to say that he'll make whatever I want once I get home.

I have to eat up as much as I can for as long as possible.

Whenever a holiday nears and my dad is told I'll be coming home, he makes a point to call to say that he'll smoke turkey wings for me once I get home. He asks me eagerly what I want to eat.

"I can make you some gumbo, Big Mike?"

He will ask me, "How those wings taste?" once they're ready and I've made my plate. He will say he got a bottle of Crown Apple for me tucked away. I drank Crown a few years ago when it first hit shelves, but I tend to drink tequila more than anything.

He'll call asking, "What's the tequila you like?" and pronounce it in a way that's not at all close to the brand.

I can barely say it myself, though.

And I usually try to pick a solid but not too pricey brand.

He'd still get it for me, but I don't want him to have to call back about the price.

He's given enough.

And he's still gonna cook for me.

The turkey wings help him say what he can't say over the phone, talking about the weather or drunkenly complaining about things he shouldn't be saying to me. He goes out of his way to make them every single time I'm home.

I can tell how happy it makes him to make them for me.

As he gets older, the happier moments are harder to come by. When he lost his brother, my uncle Terry, his grief sounded different than it had been expressed in years past. I don't have the best relationship with his family. I don't really know them.

I did know my uncle Terry. My uncle Terry is one of maybe two or three relatives from my dad's side I can say I have seen as both a child and an adult. I spoke to my dad about it. He couldn't get much out besides a sad but earnest "That was my nigga." I apologized for not being able to make his service.

I was, at the time, too broke, and too stubborn to tell him that.

Sometimes he will ask if I need some money.

"I'm just a poor Black man, but I'll give you my last."

Maybe that's his way of asking me how the writing's going?

He doesn't know my field, but he knows how hard any hustle can be.

Purpose-driven work or not, it often is very much a hustle to maintain.

Occasionally, he throws in a jab about his perceived mistreatment.

As a child, I recall a lot of his drunken rants being filled about how no one in his family listens to him. Similar rants span my adulthood. They always irritate the shit out of me. Some people don't deserve pity parties.

I love him, but I have never known him to listen as well as he speaks.

But even if we don't have a whole lot to talk about, and while it's never said between us, I think we both feel this father-and-son time on the phone—awkward and abrupt as it often is—is more time than many others get.

One friend in particular stays on my neck about how at least my dad even calls me.

I was stubborn about accepting his point, but he was right.

Buried under my banal conversations with my dad is some lingering anger and resentment.

Sometimes, father or not, I can't stand him at all.

I used to get so angry with him for all of the fucked-up shit he did and said to me, my sister, my brother, and my mother. I have raged so much that I burst into tears. I wanted to scream at him so many fucking times about it.

The resentment only lingers because there are these moments of provocation where he's a wee bit too loose with his tongue, which harkens back to that past I want to not think about anymore.

It typically happens when it's later in the day—meaning that Crown Royal, Paul Masson, and Budweiser are now directing the conversation. He will call sometimes with that. It's not something you want to hear on a random Sunday when out.

I don't think he can even help himself. He was not raised to know any better. It does not excuse his actions. But I understand the root causes better.

It's the only reason I try to talk to him. I love him and want to be respectful. For all the pain he caused, it's better to have compassion—to a point, anyway.

I just hate that the talks we have aren't always as fun and enjoyable as they could be.

He is funny. Very funny. I don't hear him laugh often, and when I do, it's more like a snicker.

A good ole country snicker. It makes him sound younger—like an innocent kid, even. I bet he's snickered like that his entire life.

I know he is insecure about his level of education, but he knows a lot more than he thinks. You don't have to know how to use a computer or the internet to be smart or clever. Since I've been around many educated people, I can confirm that a lot of them are the dumbest fucks. The world is full of overeducated people who assume they know everything because they are good at repetition. No street smarts or even common sense.

My dad has his smarts in other areas, but we never make time to talk about the futility of inferiority complexes.

We keep our conversations on the phone short and sweet.

Or maybe just enough.

As I constantly repeat to myself, it's more time than an ever-increasing amount of people in my life get with their folks.

Family is all we have.

It's too bad that we don't reminisce enough, either.

He used to take my brother and me fishing and crabbing when we were kids.

We haven't been since then, but as much as I enjoyed it back then, as an adult, you learn to appreciate things like the silence you get sitting by the water or on a bridge, doing nothing more than catching dinner. And the fryer my dad kept in the back of his old truck and used as soon as we caught enough.

I never said it was all bad. No one did. He chooses to forget that.

I know the pattern of what happens when we look backward, so I have given up. He likes to say, "Peace, I like peace." This might be as close to peace as we get. The lighter the topic, the more we stand a chance.

I know that we could probably speak at length about the music of Johnnie Taylor. If you have never heard "Disco Lady" or "Last Two Dollars," you are missing out. I keep two dollars in my wallet because of that song.

I started the habit in college and kept it going until sometime in New York City when I was too broke for words and spent it.

I am sure it was one of those times I was distant and my dad called me out of the blue to tell me not to let my pride get in the way.

That is a less desirable habit of mine.

When money got better, I fixed that.

My last two dollars in a Gucci wallet with a bee on it because of Beyoncé.

I don't think my dad even knows how much I love Beyoncé.

It's a shame that we don't talk about music. His music. My music. Our music, because even as a kid, my dad liked to keep up with what the youth listened to. He was cool that way.

That's how my few friends who have met him described him.

He likes to dance. He's quite good at it from the few times I have seen him do it. I'm certain he still has it in him.

He was cool. He is cool. But he was so menacing back then. He still is in some ways. Not so much physically anymore, but the memories remain menacing enough. He can't help but stoke them sometimes.

I love my father all the same. Even if we have to begin most of our conversations with the weather to fill the void of unresolved pain. We can't talk about his drinking peacefully, so we don't.

He is the only one who ever brings it up—and in an accusatory way against the rest of us. I want him in my life, but I don't owe him that time. That's not something I have to listen to anymore, so whenever the conversations venture in this direction, I find my escape hatch.

I try to treasure the bits where he has tried to show his capacity for change.

Like when he says "I love you" on the phone.

I'm the one who got him to say it.

I pushed for him to say it—not directly, but by my saying, "Love you, Pop"—because I know he needs to hear it. My anger at him does not mean that I don't love him. He questions my love for him at times when he does this, though.

I suppose he has witnessed too much hatred in his life to completely shake all doubts away.

But the love is evident in the effort, and I know that it applies on both ends.

We don't talk about any of this shit, of course.

He doesn't have the language.

So we talk about the weather instead.

Somehow, it is progress anyway.

Because in the end, we are both trying to stay a presence in each other's life.

If there is one additional pleasurable topic of conversation we have, and it's his asking if he needs to fuck anyone up on my behalf. That is always sweet and, yes, an indication of love.

It makes me smile because of the sentiment behind it.

He's older now, so he wants me to just get a gun already.

"You get on them papers."

I love how countrypeople talk.

A few months after I moved again, I got one of those out-of-the-blue calls from my dad.

He told me yet another friend of his had surprisingly passed.

"You got more time than me, boy," he said.

After that, he went to his usual place.

"How it feel outside, Mike?"

He has never asked me if I have a boyfriend. It's just his luck that I never have one. It would be nice if one day, while sitting on a newspaper, eating crawfish my dad boiled in the front of the house, my mom and dad would look at each other and then say to me, "Ain't you a lil' old to be in one of those situationships?" as I chew my way through the sausage and potatoes before proceeding to ironically suck the head of the crawfish after such an inquiry.

Or them asking me to bring someone around.

I am okay with neither scenario ever happening, but I do believe everyone has the capacity to surprise you. It is up to me to bring it up and bring someone around. Situations can only change with effort.

I do know my dad ultimately does not care what I'm into; I'm his son.

I have to keep trying and, when I have few words, let the weather lead the way.

My mama and I have a bit more range in terms of our conversations.

She, too, talks about the weather, but we can at least move on to other subjects.

As sick as I am of Donald Trump, old Black people hate that man with a passion that is unmatched.

Whenever my mom is about to say something that might be considered impolite, she prefaces her comments with "Lord forgive me." It's every other word when she brings Trump up. Since the 2016 presidential election, he has been a usual reference at some point in our phone conversations.

Eventually, I started to cry out, "Oh no, Mama. Not that man. Not right now. I can't."

She is more optimistic about Donald Trump going to jail than I am. Rich white men rarely go to prison. That includes the scammy white men like him.

But we'll see.

She is very much looking forward to his trials.

I tell her to turn off CNN. "It's designed to keep you riled up!" Then I tell her I need to take my own advice and turn off MSNBC.

I talk about food with her, too. I always like to gas her up on the phone about her macaroni and cheese. But really, it's the sweets she makes from scratch I most long for: her pralines, cookies, cakes, and pies. My brother and sister say that my mom only bakes to great lengths when I come home. That isn't true.

She says I just eat more of them when she does.

A godly woman, she does every so often mention me going to church. Not with the same frequency or pushiness. More like a polite nudge. I must admit, it's a shrewder strategy.

I stress to her that no matter what, I still pray—especially for her.

We have never discussed my first book, *I Can't Date Jesus*.

I never thought she would read it. I didn't think she needed to. My aunts told me that I was honest but respectful. They said as much to her.

I'm glad they felt that way. A friend and colleague of mine read my book and felt that I didn't depict my mom well. That I seemed angry with her.

A mutual friend called it conjecture and told me not to let people's troubled relationships with their parents define mine.

I love my mother more than any sentence I could ever properly convey.

I'm relieved not everyone shares that assessment of my book and feelings about my mom, but leave no room for doubt: I love her with everything in me. I always will.

My mom doesn't need to read my book to understand that, but she has read my other work over the years.

When she told me that I write so much about the mistreatment of women because of what happened to her, I smiled.

She told me that she was proud of me, and I told her how much I loved her.

She did add that she worries so much about my cynicism.

She wants me to have more faith. She says this fairly frequently, depending on my mood. Writing is a lonely experience, and I continue to stress to people that it's the career path I tripped into. And it's hard to be a writer in a climate where art is devalued.

We may not align on religion, but I am sometimes envious of how much stronger her faith makes her in times of doubt.

Before I left for LA, she told me I was still angry. I assume she meant angry with my father, but she left it open to interpretation. She was right either way.

We were speaking in person when she said it.

I didn't want to acknowledge it at the time, but we later revisited the conversation over the phone after I settled.

Instead of doing any talking, I listened to her explain that she doesn't want me to repeat her mistakes of holding on to anger for too long. She said it will make you sick. She said it can and will kill you. She said you will waste too many years of your life being angry.

"Please don't wait until your fifties like me to let go. That's one thing I didn't learn, and it almost killed me."

And some other necessary reminders.

"Give yourself a break. You're not a robot. You're not the Terminator. You're a human being."

One of those channels not named CNN had an Arnold Schwarzenegger marathon on.

All the men in my mom's life are losing their friends at a rapid rate in these last few years.

We are all struggling with it in our own ways.

My mom has used each of those losses to remind me to make more of my life by letting go of the past.

I thought I had until I was triggered by some things that evidently still tripped me up.

I have to concede that I have a lot of work left to do—and it requires work that I can't do alone.

That's why she suggested that I go to therapy.

I did not say, "You first" in response. My teeth are crooked, but it's easier to fix them if they're still there.

The first time I tried therapy, the therapist was so dismissive. He said that I just had highs and lows and would be fine. Some white man with a beard who was smug with no interest in being helpful.

My mom didn't tell me until I started writing this book that she still had to pay for the bullshit session.

I told her that I would try therapy again. That industry is dominated by people who are not Black and, more often than not, don't take insurance. It shouldn't be a luxury to date around for a therapist in order to find healing. She told me she knows how hard I'm trying.

Death has been a more dominant topic lately.

I told her at one point that I couldn't stop crying at the thought of her dying.

She knew that I was not only afraid of her dying but that she would die before I achieved enough success to feel like I could pay her back for all of the sacrifices she's made for me.

I have felt so guilty for all of those years when I was away from home. I hate that I escaped Hiram Clarke only to pursue something so lofty. I have to make this all matter more.

She keeps telling me to stop worrying about that.

That she doesn't care. I know she doesn't care. I need her to hold out for me anyway.

But this is part of her warning to me to let go and be more grateful for what has happened already in my life. And to stop being so fearful about my future. I wasn't raised to be that way.

I'm making progress on my own schedule.

We've talked about her coming to see me in LA.

She wants to see the mountains, the beaches, and experience me outside of Texas. We let too much time go by in NYC and missed the chance to do it there. Neither of us wants to let that happen again.

I tell her I will come home more often. I need to see her and the family more. I miss them. And really, I can't let more time go by.

I have wondered what will happen when I find a partner and how the conversations with my mom might go. But she's already long told me that I care too much about what she thinks and to live my life. If there's any constant with my mama, it's that she wants me to handle life better than she has, at a faster rate.

And same with how I can surprise her, she, too, might surprise me about some of those lingering what-ifs.

I have a habit of checking on my mom incessantly, reminding her to drink water while she reminds me to pray and be kinder to myself.

Part of that is loving my parents as they are for as long as I am fortunate to still have them.

I, sadly, received the scariest reminder about how precious time and life are at the beginning of 2023.

It is not my place or right to reveal specifically what's gone on, but I will say in no uncertain terms that my favorite person in the world has had to fight for her life, and I've never been more afraid of losing someone. I have never cried so much. I have never been so afraid.

At the same time, I've never found stronger faith in a person. I've never better understood how important and integral it is to have some faith in your life. To not focus on what's happened in order to better fixate on giving someone you love the support they need to conquer what's in front of them.

I was already more appreciative of my parents and treasured the growth we have been able to make together, but that love and gratitude have only gotten stronger.

I'm happy I have never given up.

That my life and our love for one another have always carried us through.

And God willing, it will carry us through this, too.

UNCLE MIKEY

No, that is not his child," my mama groaned.

We were at Hermann Hospital, and I was holding my infant niece. She does look a lot like me. It's the eyes. I've been hearing it my entire life. We all look alike.

I was fourteen when she was born, though, so my mother did not appreciate the insinuation.

It was not improbable. I had a few pregnant classmates in middle school and a whole lot more in high school. I think that maybe that's what irked her: she knew it was plausible.

Well, in theory, anyway. I'm fairly certain she had clocked me by then. Could have been praying it away.

I stifled my laughter when she said it, but howled on the inside.

The nurse who made the mistake quickly corrected herself and readjusted her tone after my mom corrected her.

That's my mom.

Incredibly polite and kind, but will get you in formation if need be.

No, the beautiful baby was not mine. It was my niece—the

perfectly age-appropriate designation for me. But she does look like me.

My sister has always pointed out that we share some personality traits. I have always been obsessed with my sister. She helped my parents with a lot of the parenting of me and my brother. It's how I knew she would be a great mom.

And I was destined to be obsessed with her children. I held my niece all of the time. It was my favorite thing to do in those years.

I spent a lot of time with her before I left for college.

I changed a lot of her diapers. I spent a lot of time watching *Teletubbies* with her. (She would later graduate to *The Cheetah Girls*.) That's my Pooh Bear—a name I jacked from her grandma.

Since my oldest niece has been old enough to text, she occasionally sends me a text on Father's Day pointing out that while I'm not her dad, she appreciates me for playing a role in her life.

My sister raised her, but I loved her as if she were mine. I think the same about her sister and my younger niece. She reminds me of my mom. Even when my oldest niece was a baby, you could tell they acted a lot alike.

It was her mannerisms.

Both my nieces look like my sister, only two separate eras of her.

But we all look alike.

Being Uncle Mikey to both has been one of the greatest blessings of my life.

And to see what my sister has done with two remarkable young women is a testament to her. My siblings and I had it harder than we should've. She never wanted that life for them. She worked incredibly hard to make sure that they didn't have that life.

They don't. They have a lightness to them that we never got to experience as kids.

I hear so much about "legacy" and how important it is to leave something behind to those who come after you.

Most mean that only in terms of wealth and assets. I want Black folks to reach economic parity, and more of us to have things to pass on to the next generation. But I also hope we leave behind more than just money and things for people. We create better environments for those who come after us. For those of us who come from cycles of abuse, we break them in order to spare other people from pain.

With my family, much as I wanted us all to make more money, I wanted the children after us to have it easier more than anything. My sister has gone beyond that, and that peace is priceless. It's a win for the future of my family.

Having said that, my youngest niece would like for me to hurry up and notch the kind of success that can put her on.

When she was six, she told me that she Googled me.

She wanted to know more about why I was on YouTube.

My youngest niece is also the first person from my family to ever wish me a happy Pride. My oldest told me she read my first book. When it was originally released, I cautioned her that she was too young to read it now, but if she ever wanted to read it, to do so when she was older. So she did.

Always sweet, she basically said that she imagined that those things couldn't have been easy for me to write, but that I was brave and she loved me.

I melted from all those texts. I don't know how to describe what it was like to "come out" to my nieces, but I can say with them, I didn't have to worry about being shunned. Neither cared. They love their uncle Mikey.

I wish more people acted like my nieces.

There's a lot of talk in this country about alphabet mafia men and children—especially in schools.

I was asked to speak at a charter school around the corner from where I attended junior high.

The teacher was younger, had read my first book, and wanted the kids to meet someone from the area.

The best way to describe it is that he was the Southern version of the Jacob Hill character from *Abbott Elementary*. But not as much of a try-hard.

He taught English, so he wanted me to talk with the kids about writing about identity along with your life and experiences.

In an email before I arrived, he told me that the students enjoyed my book. I had hoped so. Kids will confirm a lie in minutes.

I did initially wonder if I was age-appropriate since the climate suggested my existence alone was a tricky matter, but they were in high school—and I wasn't that different from some of what I was allowed to read for class back then. What I liked most about that experience was that I could tell how much it meant to see someone raised minutes away from them as a guest speaker. Same for the kids who related to me for reasons related to a shared identity. From what I could glean by their questions, anyway.

I was happy to answer—hoping to help spare them from any shame I had to experience at their age.

It was nice to be able to talk to curious students.

It's a shame that could be illegal soon in more parts of the country—including where I grew up.

What kills me about all of this chatter about "groomers" is that I have seen predators in schools my entire life.

My elementary school principal was a weird man with a creepy smile whom my mom never liked. He used to be touchy-feely in a way that registered as odd even then. He was a rubber. And he rubbed people with that odd, blank grin on his face. Like he couldn't contain himself.

My mom said to never let that man touch me.

One day at home, I heard her scream, "I knew it!" He had been arrested for trying to molest a young boy. Out of curiosity, I looked him up as an adult and found out he was now a registered sex offender.

He had that same grin on his face.

There were other creeps in middle and high school, too.

They were heterosexual men targeting young girls, but they belonged in a holding cell with the creepy principal.

None of those Republicans speak out about that kind of grooming.

Queer men are not the threat to children some make us to be, though I have let those stigmas seep into my own consideration of having children.

I already worry that I am too rusty with babies and small kids. My nieces are older now, so I haven't been around children that young in some years. More of my friends started to have children. I get to test if the connection is there.

One of my friends, Candy, had talked about her desire to become a mom when I first lived in LA. A decade later, she was now living her dream. When I went to meet her beautiful baby, I held her, and to my delight, she was calm with me, and I held her the entire time—including when her mom went to cook.

"Look at how much Cheyanne loves her uncle Mikey."

That was the hope.

I told her, "This almost makes me want one."

She encouraged it, but when I asked if she still wanted all these kids like she used to, she said no.

"I'm too old now."

I was older than her.

I will always laugh at my mom's immediate response to me telling her that I was gay being "Well, I guess I won't have any more grandchildren."

I told her that didn't mean I wouldn't have any.

I can surprise her.

Like the time that I decided to join my sister, my nieces, and my mama at Christmas mass.

I hadn't been inside of a Catholic church in well over a decade.

I did not catch on fire as I stepped inside, but I did catch my mom off guard when I asked if I could join them. She played it cool, but my sister was not convinced.

"She fronting, you know she happy you're coming!"

My brother came, too. We hadn't been together in that way in an incredibly long time. There we were together in the name of Jesus with a new generation of Christians. I bet inside she was ecstatic. I was fine.

We were at St. Benedict the Abbot Catholic Church, where I was baptized and which was only a few minutes away from my mom's house.

I noticed some of the prayers and dialogue had been updated.

The priest was Black but from some other country. The attendees were mostly Black and Latino immigrants. So many people my age have fled Catholicism. There weren't that many people there, and this was the Christmas Eve service.

Have the heathens won?

I went to make my mom happy. She always talks about needing to hold on until at least my youngest niece is off to college. I don't like when she talks about her death. I wonder what she might say if I decide to have kids.

I want her around as long as God will allow it though I won't ask her to hold on until college—but she'd be happy to know that no matter what, I'll make sure my baby has a baptism. A Black child needs every blessing they can get in this world.

My sister once told me that she could see me being a good dad. I would like to think I have the capacity to be one. I do wonder as I get older if I will ever take the real plunge.

Kids are expensive as hell, and there is a premium placed on my community based on the mechanics of procreation.

Could I do it alone? I write for a living. Perhaps it would be more ideal to have a partner/cosigner. Then I wonder whether I will even have the option.

I'm writing this under the rule of a Supreme Court with a conservative majority inclined to make same-sex marriage and sodomy illegal while permitting greater discrimination against us based on religious grounds. It might soon be illegal to even have a baby the expensive way. Will I have to go underground and take up on those offers to have a baby with one of my homegirls?

People who want to have children should. Gay parents who can afford to ought to do it. Republicans push me in the direction of fatherhood with their hate campaign, but having children to be spiteful is for the straights.

I have my doubts, but I just know I can be a better dad than the men maligning me.

Being a gay uncle is not the same thing as being a father, but it's a good-enough preview of my capacity to be caring and loving to a child. To make them feel safe, loved, and valued. To show them how to be a decent and kind person.

Of all the new fake holidays that spring up on social media, my favorite is on August 14th. It is Gay Uncle's Day. It will never be as big as the parental days, but we're owed some kind of recognition now that our reputation is being tarnished out there. I don't need a gift or a tax write-off. The smiles on my nieces' faces whenever I see them will suffice.

Very few things sound better to me than their saying "Uncle Mikey."

It remains to be seen if I'll ever be anyone's father, but in the meanwhile, I increasingly tell my sister how happy I am that she's made me an uncle. I've learned so much about myself—including how much love and joy I can give to children even if I never have my own. It's a pride no one can take from me.

I FINALLY BOUGHT SOME JORDANS

There is no nice way of asking a person, "Are you still poor?"
Not that some people won't try.

Admittedly, she didn't phrase it that way *exactly*, but I picked up on what was being put down.

She wanted to know how poor I felt that day.

I was doing a promotional interview for my second book with a radio station based in Amsterdam.

As she explained over Zoom, she was surprised to read that my student loan debt remained such a financial burden in my life after the release of my first book.

She wanted to know the status of my debt now that I have another one out and maybe a TV show coming (heavy emphasis on the "maybe").

Following a couple of other interviews with the European press, I have gotten used to their pity masked as questions. Say, "What's it like to worry about getting shot in a mass shooting every day of your life?" Or "Why is your healthcare system so stupid and evil?" Student loan debt existed where she lived, but not at the scale I wrote about. She said as much, hence her worry.

But folks worried over here, too.

After the release of that book, people have written to me about their own struggles with student loan debt. I got a few nobody-told-you-to-do-that responses, too. Generally, though, those who read the book and reached out to me were hoping that I no longer felt like my life was being strangled by my student loans.

So she was coming from a good place, albeit I wasn't sure how I wanted to answer.

Writing about it is one thing; speaking openly about it with a stranger is another.

I answer questions honestly, but while I didn't write the book to be pitied, I didn't share my story to be scolded, either. That happened in one particular radio interview. As amusing as it is to be lectured by someone who doesn't know what they're talking about, it's a waste of minutes better spent just trying to gauge interest in the book. I can't control the people underselling me and the industries designed to undercut me. I do the best I can with the conditions that I have been dealt. That was the point of the book—reaching that place in my life.

After that experience, I learned to be more selective with which questions to answer.

In this case, I answered in a way I felt most comfortable with at that moment.

The loans don't have me in the poorhouse like they used to.

It was a satisfying-enough answer for the both of us.

She followed by asking about capitalism in the age of the pandemic. Something about whether I felt socialism is a better model and some other questions that felt way too early in the day in my time zone to talk about. I said that I understood and agreed with the underlying point in the framing of her question—capitalism is bad—but noted that as far as facilitating death goes, if you look around, various nations with different types of governments are equally guilty of lying to their people and letting their citizens die. I found it genuinely depressing to think about and wanted to shift away from the topic and other questions that reminded me of those college debate scenes in *Power Book II: Ghost*. It's no shade; she did a fine interview. I don't like the system as it is, either, but I don't see it changing anytime soon.

I ended by pivoting back to the book, saying my best way to deal with capitalism at this point in my life was to crawl out of debt as fast as possible.

The plague did impact me financially, as I wasn't able to physically go outside and make money as I had planned to, but I was fortunate to be able to continue working from home.

It was not the year I planned for, but the end result was feeling more financially secure in that I was able to make my payments, big as they remained, on time. That was only comforting to me for a few months. Unless I dropped a sizable portion of that debt, my life wouldn't change much. I'd always have that in the back of my head. I decided to take on as much work as possible for as long as I could manage.

I took on as many writing assignments as I could find. I was also doing speaking engagements when I could. I was not sure how well I performed from my living room. There's only so much you can glean from the corner of your eye as you talk and people leave comments.

I first started to pay off my credit card debt and then moved to my student loans one by one.

These were not small amounts of money. I still owed tens of thousands in student loans.

Little by little I knocked the smallest loans out, and in spite of providing some nominal relief, I didn't make a real difference until I was paid for the pilot of my first failed TV development project. I did not hit the lottery, but the check for that script was the largest check I had ever received for a single bit of work. Even if I was disappointed by the outcome, this was enough to get me past the biggest financial burden of my life.

I am not totally debt-free. I have one private loan left with a low balance and two government loans. But as far as the nuisance in my life, my main lender, Citibank, and later, Discover Student Loans, I was done with them forever.

No more of their calls, letters, emails, and texts. No more reminders of what might happen to me (and my mama) if I didn't find the money to settle the balance before the loan went into default. No more worries of that happening and confirming my suspicions that my career was a selfish pursuit.

I am so happy to say I don't have to deal with them anymore.

Not that they made it easy.

The internet in the Airbnb I took up space in for months had glitchy Wi-Fi every now and then.

So there I was, a pivotal moment of my life—paying these annoyingly evil people off.

When I tried to make the final payment, I initially didn't think it had gone through.

The page wouldn't load.

Okay.

I can scroll back.

Refresh.

Let's try again.

Oh, that's strange . . . it's doing the same thing.

For once, it was not this janky internet. Everything else was working fine. I was a little frustrated, but I tried again. You have to understand. I had spent years of my life stressing about these loans.

I stuck my fingers down my throat to feel some semblance of control over my life in response to the pressure of carrying these loans. I had denied myself joy so many times out of guilt for having these loans. This company was going to take my fucking money when I was trying to give it to them. This moment was going to happen.

I was going to get my confirmation number.

Finally.

I got to my knees, had my moment, and got up and went about my day.

A little anticlimactic, but no less satisfying. Until I went to the site the next day and saw the full amount I owed still on the screen. But multiple charges in the same amount for what I paid the day before. A few minutes after that, I got one of their emails about the payment due date approaching.

Incensed, I called the lender's customer service line only to be sent in multiple directions for two hours.

I eventually got to talk to a human being and was told to basically prove it. They couldn't see it on their side, the customer service rep explained to me. "No record of it at all. It may show up soon! You never know!"

I was not leaving a chance to these evil people.

"We can't give back what we don't see," she explained in a haughty tone.

Like it was her money.

I try not to lose my patience with underpaid customer service representatives for multinational corporations, but these were the same people who harassed me on Christmas Eve for payment.

They wanted one more shakedown.

The payment was over six thousand dollars, so I was going to prove it.

I went to my mom, who of course owns a printer, and sent them their proof so they could credit my account and let us be done with each other. Days later, after I sent a printout of my checking account as proof of payment, the next call was more pleasant.

In about twelve years, I had paid over six figures in debt, plus interest.

As for the remaining loans, I forgot that when you pay off a large amount of debt in a short amount of time and the account closes, your credit score takes a temporary tumble. So better to pace myself, but that last private one will be gone soon. I'm taking my time on those government ones out of spite; they should have been canceled, anyway.

As all of this happened, the rent, already too high, got higher. As did gas. And chicken wings. And basically everything.

But when I told my friend about getting Discover Student Loans away from me, she eagerly congratulated me and suggested that I buy something nice for myself.

I didn't immediately think of buying anything after I paid my loans . . . and then got my lender to acknowledge that I paid my loans.

That thought hadn't even crossed my mind.

After college, I'd treat myself to something nice every now and again. I was working. I was feeling responsible. I was trying to show myself—and perhaps everyone else—how despite debt and its deep, deep frustrations, I was fighting. Everything became about the loans or medical bills or tax bills or trying to help others whenever possible.

Before that second book, my struggles with those loans were the harshest.

I fell into the mentality that I didn't deserve nice things because of the struggles.

"You shouldn't have thought that way to begin with. But your life is different now, isn't it?" my friend asked me. "Do something to celebrate that."

My mind went back to how I originally grew up feeling priced out of a lot.

When I was a kid, there were few things I wanted more than a Starter jacket. Two in particular: the Charlotte Hornets, with its classic turquoise, and the Orlando Magic—the black boosted by drops of dark blue and white. I might have been in denial about a few things back then, but my colors? I knew and accepted those.

Starter jackets signified a certain degree of early-nineties cool, a cool I would later come to understand as status. In order to look a certain way—expensive, and whatever else suggests better than others—you need to be able to afford your bragging rights.

I loved Starter jackets, but when I used to hear about folks getting shot over them, it never made sense to me. You're going to threaten to kill someone over a jacket in Texas? I didn't get that, but I wanted one, anyway.

My jackets and coats were from deeply discounted department stores. The clothes were . . . not always it. They weren't like what the other kids were wearing to school.

This was in no way a knock to my parents.

I never wanted for what I needed, and that is what will always matter.

Nevertheless, other folks know how to make you feel excluded.

Those jackets lost their appeal with time, but I felt the same way about Jordans, too.

I remember the days of wearing Payless Shoes in elementary.

By middle school, though, my sister took the lead by using her money to make us, her little brothers, look better at the feet. We had Air Maxes, shoes from other NBA players like Penny Hardaway and Grant Hill, but never Jordans.

The only time I tried to get some—what would now be the Air Jordan 11 Retros—they were sold out. I wanted some Js since elementary, and when I finally felt like I could get them on my own, they were sold out. All I got that day from Sharpstown Mall was Mrs. Fields Cookies.

I told someone I had planned to get them, and when I came back to school without them, as silly as it might sound, it stoked my biggest insecurities about feeling priced out.

In later years, I felt priced out of vacations, relationships, home ownership, and so much other stuff thanks to the debt I carried. With a big chunk of my debt erased, I felt like I was moving into a situation where everything didn't feel so unattainable if I just kept going. So I did think I should treat myself in some way that alleviated that feeling of being priced out of everything.

I thought about a specific kind of car, but quickly changed my mind. Let me sell a TV show first; let it make at least a second season before doing that. And don't be new somewhere in these times with a car that screams, "Carjack me" in a city you don't know well enough.

Once my credit score rebounded from the jolt of a bunch of lines and credit being abruptly closed, I started getting mail and messages about a mortgage loan. I crawled out of debt, and here came the setup for the next load.

I knew better than to dream about buying a house. In California? Or anywhere outside of Texas?

To the disappointment of Black folks who scream about "generational wealth," I am in no rush to be a homeowner.

I don't see it as a key to wealth given that unless I live in a white neighborhood and put pictures of white people in the house should I want to sell it, the property will be regarded as less valuable. In all likelihood, if I do buy a home, I'll be living around Black people—so by default, the home will be valued less. And depending on where I live, I have to factor in climate change and where we're usually relegated to in a given city.

I do see the benefits from my friends who are homeowners. I recognize that with regard to rent control, a mortgage is the kind of rent stabilization laws don't generally provide anymore. I also see a lot of responsibilities and taxes that I don't want to pay yet. Not until I decide on where I firmly want to spend the next chapter of my life in a thirty-year-mortgage kind of way.

That said, I want all of the Black people who want to be home-owners to buy homes. I salute you. Congratulations on getting away from a landlord in this economy. Root for me that I may one day join you. Just don't sell it to me as a key to wealth building.

I wish wealth wasn't the goal being sold to us.

I want financial security. I want to be able to help people and causes I care about. I want freedom from the type of depression financial insecurity lends to people. I know I have to attain the kind of success that's harder than ever to secure.

I sometimes struggle with people telling me that they are proud of me.

I do all right, but I'm not rich. I worry about my earning po-tential never reaching its full potential. Another writers strike. More media consolidation—an outcome rarely good for minority creatives. While writing this book, I got an invitation for what was described as "your conversational AI partner."

Some advice given is better than others.

"You need to go see Oprah," a nosy white woman cleaning my teeth said to me after asking me what I did for a living.

She said if she were me, she would get in my car and drive right up to Oprah's house. My book titles sounded "interesting," so that should do the trick. It must be nice to be that delusional.

I prefer my counsel from those I actually know.

"You worry too much" and "I don't worry about you" are the usual responses I get when I bring some of this up.

And when it came to the challenge of treating myself, my friend was relentless.

"Here you go overthinking shit. I didn't say buy that car or look up a townhome. I said, 'Get something nice.'"

Sometimes I worry that some of what that debt stole from me includes potential that can't be recaptured. But that is me over-thinking shit. My worries about being behind blind me to the reality that success often comes in increments. I had to stop allowing myself to fall into the thinking that my victories aren't worth celebrating, and in this, rewarding myself for accomplishing a big feat.

Without major purchases on my horizon to signify my life changed, I looked for a less anxiety-inducing purchase. Something that no longer felt like I was priced out of.

I'm but a country Black man, so I decided the way to celebrate my win is to be a nigga and buy some shoes.

I got on the SNKRS app and finally bought some Jordans.

I'm so late in joining you, active sneakerheads, but the SNKRS app is hell. Most of what I wanted was gone, but I did find one pair I liked. For the first time in a long time, I was able to spend money and not feel guilty about a student loan bill.

These sneakers were not the ones I couldn't get at Sharpstown.

I have decided to buy that pair—the Air Jordan 11 Retros—once this book is released into the world. Just as another treat to myself. But the ones I did buy that day, and some others I bought not long after, were less stressful purchases as opposed to tackling what initially came to mind.

Perhaps it's the silliest thing to find so much joy in something so small and insignificant, but I do. By heeding my friend's challenge, besides getting the shoes, I learned that I don't need to feel priced out, left behind, or not all the way caught up.

I'm where I need to be, and even if incremental, there are positive changes happening in my life as a result of my pursuits.

I may not always feel that way, but if I only look up, I can see it all around me.

Down to my feet.

A LOVELY VIEW OF A BURNING WORLD

I came back to LA with simple goals: to heal and to make TV money.

I learned the value of patience and the perks of sometimes moving slower after leaving New York, but after pushing back my moving date repeatedly over the course of several months while in Houston, I eventually decided that it was time for me to get on with my life and move.

I was happy to be back in Houston for a while. Being absent for so long outside of the one or two visits for holidays had weighed on me. I wanted to rectify that at a time of sickness and seclusion. It was an opportunity to enjoy as much time with my family as much as possible. So many people I love deeply didn't have the same option. I needed to not take these moments for granted any longer.

While there, I was reminded of the reason(s) that kept me away. But I don't have any regrets about going back for a while or sticking around longer than I had originally planned. I settled on the notion that I needed to see and hear and feel it all—even some of those difficult moments.

I love my city and my family, but home is never a hundred-percent calm. Maybe it never will be. The root of a lot of the pain I have carried is there. I've been reminded repeatedly over my adult life that my problems will follow me everywhere, but I used that time to try and learn to accept what can and will not change. And to love anyway.

I promised to go home more often and have measured expectations, but I still had a dream to pursue and some healing on my own left to do.

Before any of that could begin in earnest, though, I first needed to find a new place to live.

The whole trip was supposed to be about finding an apartment, but it instantly became more about seeing people I hadn't seen in two years. Outside of my immediate family and friends I could count on my hand, I had not been around people in almost two years at that point.

I had forgotten what it was like to be social. I was excited. And keeping with my mission, I ended up working more than I assumed I would as well.

But then I told everyone to please let me focus and find a home.

It is not easy to find an apartment in a city like LA when you aren't physically present. Initially, a friend referred me to someone who said she could help. And to her credit, she tried to when I hit her up—a couple of months before I actually flew out there.

As I told her, those coronavirus rates were mighty high out there; I might have to wait.

So I did, but by the time I arrived and looked for her, she ghosted me the entire week.

I was there for work and planned to spend a few days with her searching for a place.

Oh well.

I knew that if I left LA without finding a place to live, it would only delay my plans even more. I did not fly out there for naught, so I took about thirty-six hours to make something happen as best I could.

I only had a few simple requirements.

Parking was an absolute must; I was not fighting for a space on a public street. Life is too short.

A refrigerator, which for some reason is not guaranteed for Los Angeles rentals.

Air-conditioning, duh. Dry heat is heat.

Most of all, space. I deserved space.

LA has a surprisingly high number of roaches. They are everywhere. It is so disgusting. I'm never going back to that. The same goes for rats.

The city has a higher number of rats than often advertised, but it's been my experience that they are relegated to specific regions of the city, like Downtown. I've never been that fond of Downtown LA. When I first lived in LA, I noticed how a lot of the area was being remade into what kind of looked like a fake NYC. A decade later, it looks even more like that—now offering larger and grander versions of New York apartments that, yes, are expensive but, when compared to New York rental prices, somewhat of a deal. That is not an endorsement of the rent in either city, by the way—someone needs to fry up the rich or, at the very least, skewer some of those landlords and get more affordable housing going.

I had not planned to live Downtown, but it was suggested to me. It's nice to visit, but Downtown LA reminds me of Gotham City. Whenever I am down there, I fear that at any moment I am going to have to stop and fight the Riddler.

My mama did hand me a taser for the road, but I'd rather not.

And again, rats.

I have seen enough on the street.

No, thank you.

I found my place on a walk from my hotel. Much as I love running, after experiencing sciatic nerve pain while in Texas, I run a lot less than I used to. Aging is crueler than it needs to be.

Walks are cool, too, though. I can confirm that I'm now one of those people who counts their steps. In addition to working out, I try to hit at least ten thousand steps a day.

I like walks for non-health obsessed reasons, too.

Ever since I left NY, I have been asked if I miss it.

Not especially, but after a while, I did miss parts of it—like the ability to move around and see the city.

That's not a big thing in LA, but I recommend it—and it's even better to take a walk and smoke a pre-roll when you can't smoke in your hotel room.

I was staying in Koreatown, an area I lived in for a bit the first time I came to Cali.

It had to have been at least a decade since I walked down this particular street.

I used to go to a gym in the area, so I was familiar.

It was as loud a street as I remember. One key difference was the sight of multiple new buildings and many more in waiting. You couldn't help but notice all of the construction going on—or the homeless people sleeping around it.

Homelessness has always been a problem in Los Angeles, but as someone who first visited LA way back in 2002, I couldn't recall ever seeing it this bad.

I noticed the difference immediately once I left the airport and was taken to my hotel. As soon as we hit the 405, there it was: people living on the side of the freeway, under the freeway, and on the freeway's overpass. It looked worse than ever in Hollywood as well, and for that matter, wherever I went on this trip.

Even on the street I was walking on at the moment.

California sells itself as some liberal bastion, but I have always thought of the place as more like a stuck-up version of Texas.

I kept being asked what Texas was like whenever someone asked to look at my ID.

I couldn't say, "My mama don't want y'all down there. It causes too much traffic," so I went with "Kind of like LA, only without Hollywood and with humidity that will eventually feel painful."

I wished them all luck on their pursuits of states with lower costs of living; they wished me good luck finding a place to rent that wouldn't leave me feeling hopeless and destitute.

LA is a pretty place to live so long as you can afford to. I feel sorry for those who increasingly can't.

This is, after all, the city where I was once cursed to die poor.

And to be blunt, when I first drove away, I was sleeping on someone's couch.

Can't lose this time, I thought.

I'm so close.

Only a few minutes into my walk did I look up and see a building that looked like a nice place to live.

It was the first place that looked decent enough.

It was right by some kind of religious institution—I thought a church, but perhaps it was a synagogue? There was not a lot of marking, but I knew it was holy. It made me think of my old block in Harlem that had the small church with the loud choir full of members right with God, but not the notes.

I called to make an appointment to see the apartment building the next day and decided to enjoy the high and continue walking.

When I arrived to visit the building, the building manager asked what I did for a living as he showed me around.

I told him I wrote books and on the internet, but ideally, one or both of my books could at least become a TV show before Hollywood forgot that Black and/or gay people were alive.

He smiled politely, presumably thinking in his head, *Another writer—I'm definitely going to need to see his tax returns.*

The building felt peaceful and the unit he showed me matched that vibe. I was interested and in a time crunch, so I asked him where I could apply for the unit. I hadn't applied for an apartment in several years. The problems with self-employment are bountiful, though in my case, even if I was in a better place financially, a tiny bit of me worried in the back of my mind if past mistakes might block new blessings.

I had managed to pay off all but one of my private student loans, but that did not take off the years of late payments nor the initial hits to your score once you clear those loans off. And by the time I viewed this apartment, much of America had already backtracked on its pledges to help Black people. Their guilt did not get me into this apartment—my credit score, tax statements, and eagerness to pay up to secure the unit did.

Once I got the apartment, I made plans to drive myself to LA for another journey.

It turns out a few of the friends I met in NYC who had moved to LA relocated to Koreatown, too.

One of the first people I showed my new apartment to quickly noted that a few known TikTok creators lived in my building. I smiled and said, "I'm sure they do." The only thing I had noticed about my neighbors in the early days was that most only talk to one another if they have dogs. That and there were some but not many Black people around.

I am used to living in Black neighborhoods, but that's not yet happened for me in Los Angeles. I would like that to change should I stay longer. In the meanwhile, I nod to the Black people whenever I spot them in my building and clock the ones who don't respond in kind.

I can't trust you if you don't nod.

It's been nice not to be awakened in the middle of the night by the brown liquor–induced tirades of an upset person directed at her partner. That alone was worth the hike in rent. I do resent hearing the helicopters every so often at odd hours of the night, but I can't fault the building for giving the LAPD the kind of budget where they can fly helicopters all day and all night.

I now live about five minutes or so from my first and second apartments in LA. The second, much better than the first, was the place that I had to give up after I was owed so much money that I could barely handle my share of the rent, much less the other room that was then vacated.

I have those final months burned into my memory. I couldn't forget it if I tried. Judging from the multiple notices that went up on the doors of a number of units the second after LA County dropped its eviction moratorium, I best never keep them waiting on rent, lest they toss me outside.

One day, I hope I can live like Marcus Graham in the original *Boomerang*.

For right now, I simply want to feel comfortable in my own space.

It occurred to me months into my move that I hadn't ever lived in a space that I was totally comfortable living in for one reason or another.

For the first time, I was living somewhere that didn't cause or house anxiety.

I felt proud of that moment once my place started to come more together and feel like my home.

As for LA itself, there were so many LA transient clichés that I skipped my first time there.

I had no intention of repeating that mistake.

In addition to walking, I am very into hiking now.

I love being the person who can now talk about loving to go on hikes.

I hike, and I drink matcha oak-milk lattes—with vanilla. It is delightful. Not often, though. I am predisposed to diabetes, and America has already proven that it will let me drop dead in future plagues, so I try not to give her any advantages.

In addition to work and healing, I have other goals.

I want to be a bad bitch inside and out.

Let me add the following disclaimer before the declaration sparks concern: I already know that I'm a bad bitch, so, yes, what I really mean is all I want in this life is to become a *badder* bitch.

When my friend Candy referred me to a trainer named Ryan, he asked me what my goals were. I said to have the male equivalent of a specific R & B's singer's breast implants. He needed a moment to process that, but after he thought about it and got a visual in mind, he told me I was funny.

After that, I added that as much as I was driven by vanity, I needed to feel more in control of my own body. I wasn't really chasing an unattainable body standard; I was ready to settle for the grand prize of substantially less body dysmorphia. Working out with Ryan helped with that and subsequently allowed me to develop more useful habits to deal with stress, anxiety, and other tensions.

I wanted to adhere to my mama's advice not to hold on to so much needless anger, as you not only will waste so much of the precious time, but it might also kill you.

I don't want to walk around with a hot head.

After all, I am an Aries.

I don't exactly know what that means, but astrology has a choke hold on anyone under the age of forty-five, so it has been at least relayed to me that if you're an Aries, you bring the fire. I do recognize that boxing has helped me better channel such energy and, overall, helped me learn to be more in control of my body.

Speaking of flames, I have been asked by many—especially family—why I would move to a state that always catches on fire.

Well, my love of NYC notwithstanding, besides that city's brutal winters, the rats, the cost of living, and the mayor who behaves more like a club promoter, I see videos of a subway system that can't handle a rainstorm, much less any future hurricanes.

I won't drown with rats, nor will I wait on my Uber to get me out of a storm's path.

I could end up back in Houston, but not only does the city have to worry about hurricanes the hotter it gets, a once-in-a-generation winter storm that now happens yearly might take the grid out.

No matter where I go, the planet might take me out.

In LA, at least I have a lovely view of a burning world.

I like Koreatown, but it doesn't necessarily provide the best views of Los Angeles. What sold me on my apartment building was that after I overshared a bit about my past here and elsewhere, I said that I wanted to find a place that made me feel like I really lived in LA. He answered that by making sure the patio in my place allowed me to see the Griffith Observatory.

If the fires get close, I can drive away, but until then, I want to take in how beautiful this place is and hope it inspires me to create something beautiful while here.

I didn't make it back to LA until at least two years after my initial plan.

Slowly, painfully, and ever so stubbornly, I'm learning to accept that I never get anything I want on my schedule. Things happen when they are supposed to.

Some people like to say that you choose happiness. I have always found this sentiment to be infuriating. To me, it's too blanket of a statement that feels unfair to people living with pain.

Some of us inherit a lot of other folks' unresolved trauma, pain, and anger before we even speak our first words. A lot of us don't even realize it until well into our adulthoods. You can't simply will away pain or depression with words—no matter how loudly you shout them at yourself.

What you can do in terms of choice is to try. Not everyone tries or tries hard enough, but giving people grace and space is more encouraging than saying you can snap your misery away.

Life can get better, but it takes a long time for a lot of us to get to that place.

I thought I was getting there when I moved to LA. My friends there and elsewhere noted there was something different about me. That I had a lightness to me.

Then I lost my friend Brian to brain cancer, and it triggered more sadness and grief. I had lost so many people in a short amount of time, but that loss was especially painful because he was one of the very first people with whom I ever shared who I was. So many people had been unkind to me for reasons like that, but never him. I loved him so much. I still love him.

He was the kind of friend I had hoped to see more now that I felt less bogged down by debt. He was the kind of good friend I had hoped to grow old with. I'm so tired of losing people I expected to be around for the long haul.

My grief over his loss gave way to other grief that had been dormant. I was beginning to once again feel angry, sad, and sometimes hopeless about the future.

I felt that lightness slipping away and found myself regressing. I felt myself drowning after a while.

I don't like admitting how much pain I'm in. That I still carry more grief, worry, and sometimes rage than I should at this age. That I sometimes smoke too much in order to numb the pain. That perhaps some are right, and I'm just not trying hard enough.

I knew what I wanted this book to be when I first sold it.

It wasn't about making it in terms of money or a certain tier of success. My intent was to share that after dealing with cycles of abuse and economic woes, I was managing to overcome it all and get closer to becoming the man I knew I could be. Unfortunately, I don't have the happiest ending I initially envisioned for this, which is why I struggled so much to write it.

There is no one thing that has managed to snap me out of that place. I just had to keep trying. Again and again and again. I wake up every day with the intent to make it a good one.

Some of my scars may never go away. And I may always be triggered by loss or triggered whenever I put myself in certain environments. But I can still be happy so long as I keep going and trying. And measure my expectations while accepting what I can and can't control.

All of that work has not been in vain.

In that context, that remains progress for me.

I never needed to tie a pretty bow on this book as a means to bridge my first two. Life is hard. It's harder than it should be for some of us. Even when it's good. Even when you feel fortunate.

Many days, I don't feel like I know what the hell I am doing anymore.

Everything has changed since the pandemic. I am trying to remind myself of what my purpose is and what I want my life to be in the future. At the same time, I sometimes am growing tired of constantly having to prove my value. In both my professional life and personal life, I have had to contend with prejudices and biases, but when working in fields that already greatly devalue a writer, there is a premium, and people like me pay it.

I worry if I will get tired of paying it sooner rather than later.

I have considered making some changes should that happen.

Much as I have appreciated my writing career, it always feels like every industry I enter wants to haze me. My work is a privilege to do, but it is work, and you can always change what you do.

I can do anything that doesn't require me ever paying tuition again.

My life will work out no matter what. I don't want work stressing me out in the ways it used to. I'm happy so many Americans are recognizing that and quitting their jobs accordingly—the ones who can afford to, at least.

I'm not totally sure of my future, but I want it to be peaceful. I will never stop fighting for my peace. I've been told recently that once I turn forty, much of these anxieties will go away.

Everything isn't perfect, but I am hopeful that will be the case soon enough.

Los Angeles, whatever you think about it, is a city too sunny for me to ever stay too mad for too long. Part of my more recent struggles was rooted in me not completely letting go of the past. I want this book to be the last bit of that. I don't need to cling to that hurt anymore. There is enough around me trying to break my soul.

Like America, the empire is in its flop era.

The political climate is dumber and more hateful than ever, as we have an entire political party actively trying to stomp the existence out of people like me. It would be my luck that I find love and success in telling my story right as sodomy is outlawed again. I'll be ready to break the law regardless.

We'll see, but for now, I want to enjoy my life as much as I can for as long as I can.

And like I said, enjoy a lovely view of a burning world as I navigate this next stage of my life.

I wish things were easier, but I'm starting to feel lighter again and ready for what's to come.

I have to believe that so long as I keep trying, the rest will fall into place, that I will finally have my peace.

I told myself that if it didn't work out for me after a while, I could move to Atlanta next and write hood lit novels or something.

Perhaps befriend a *Real Housewives of Atlanta* cast member, too, and see where else life takes me.

It would have more views of hookah lounges than hills, but I'd make due.

FORGIVE ME, BEYONCÉ, FOR I HAVE SINNED

My friend Maiya once said that we'll know we're old when I can't get low anymore.

I have Houston knees, but there have been other signs.

While playing bingo for money with kin at my cousin's house for Christmas, one of the younger cousins made a joke about my eldest niece being old now, ". . . like thirty-seven."

I immediately started laughing.

My niece informed him that I was thirty-seven.

"Wow, you don't look it. But my bad. It's not *really* old."

It's not so much a benefit, but I have learned that gay people often dive into ageism early. I'm not sure if it's life expectancy for the demo or what, but as soon as I turned twenty-five, I would hear about how much older I was getting. The benefit to experiencing ageism that early is that I'm relatively numb to it now.

Relatively.

I felt confident in my skin regimen, but not enough to forget I just got smacked up the head with the word of my declining youth from the actual youth.

But he had a nice recovery, and while not required, it was very much appreciated.

I told him it was cool and not to let my old ass get in the way.

After that was cleared up, I called bingo and grabbed my cane in order to walk over and collect my winnings.

It could have been much worse: he could have described me as someone born in "the 1900s."

It makes me laugh as much as it does elicit irrational rage. I truly try not to heckle and boo Gen Z the way some actual mean old people do, but whenever I hear a Gen Z person say "born in the 1900s," I imagine them falling through a trapdoor. Must they say it like that?

I reserve the same level of contempt for "geriatric millennial."

If I could fight that turn of phrase, I would kick it in the face the way Shawn Michaels used to. Then find a way to leap into the air and further elbow it into the ground like the late "Macho Man" Randy Savage. I will not accept it.

Dig it?

Call me old. Again, I've been hearing jokes about that since I turned twenty-five. They feel better when delivered with the backhanded compliment that I "don't look my age," but I understand that I am technically now middle-aged.

When I got back to LA and went to meet a friend at a bar in West Hollywood, they did not ask to see my ID to get into the bar I was invited to.

I see my visible signs of aging.

"Don't you start fucking with your face now that you're out there" were the first words Jade, a friend of mine, said to me when she called once I settled in LA.

It never came to mind, though I have tried microneedling.

I had forgotten that it used to be called a vampire facial but remembered as soon as the procedure began. I don't know if I would try that again. Depends on how strong and quick the numbing cream around is.

But this is the kind of LA shit I wanted to do . . . within reason.

I don't mind my frown lines, so I won't be trying Botox. Don't you have to keep paying for that? I will drink water and pray over some Korean face masks before putting them on my face.

One slight complaint I have about getting older is that when COVID shut down the world, a good chunk of my thirties was taken from me.

When enough of the pandemic died down, I wanted to make good on lost time.

Growing up, I used to go to a lot of concerts and would often see that at certain concerts, there would be a noticeable amount of old heads you wouldn't expect to be there having the time of their lives.

I have been waiting my whole life to become that brand of old head at a concert.

One thing I appreciate about my friend dré is that, like me, he couldn't wait to be the old person at a concert, too.

Now that outside had opened back up, it was time for me to fulfill my destiny.

It was a last-minute invite, but when dré texted me asking if I wanted to go see Azealia Banks, I said, "Whew . . . the devil. Count me in."

Was this the concert equivalent of ordering a Chick-fil-A combo? Depends on who you ask and what she's done or said that week. But like I'll dip a Christian fried-chicken nugget in some sweet sriracha every now and again, I wasn't turning this free ticket down. The show reminded me of why I used to root for her so hard. And no matter what's happened to her over the years, she remains a star, as evidenced by her having the entire theater literally jumping throughout her show.

When she said something about Lizzo's weight, I turned to my friend and was like, "See . . ."

dré noted at one point that we were the oldest people in the room.

I told him that felt right.

I wouldn't say we were the oldest people at the Latto concert—perhaps the oldest without children.

Latto is around the same age as one of my nieces, but I'm as big a fan of Latto as my nieces are . . . if not more. Latto's album *Queen of Da Souf* helped me so much in the early 2020s.

When I heard her rap, "I love me a country-ass nigga with some gold teeth," I felt seen and heard.

So when dré asked if I wanted to go, I once again emphatically said yes.

Proof that old habits die hard, as soon as I walked into the Peacock Theater, the somewhat surprisingly diverse crowd was already going thanks to a DJ. Some lady rushed me and immediately started twerking on me. I was supposed to be heading to my seat with the friends I came with, but I didn't want to be rude. I danced along.

Suddenly, I heard, "Where did Michael go?"

Then an arrow was pointed at me on the ground, dancing.

I got back up and excused myself, but that felt nice. I felt like my old self. I could have shed a happy tear. I was among my people.

Most of all, I could get up.

Thank you for not giving up on me, knees.

I don't know how old she thought I was, but it made me think of the lit OGs in my own life and the ones I aspire to become.

I keep stretching with the hopes to fully live up to their legacy.

I have to live up to their legacy, so I make sure I keep stretching.

I'm older now, not fucking geriatric.

Once we got to our seats, I noticed that for all the doom and gloom of the news, not only did people want to party, but you could see progress onstage and in the crowd.

By now I was full of tequila and popping Camino gummies, but I perked up for the opening act, Saucy Santana.

Lil Nas X had already become the first gay Black male pop star thanks to "Old Town Road" and subsequent hits like "MONTERO (Call Me By Your Name)," so the unthinkable was already made possible. I hate that he ultimately continues to contend with the dumbest forms of homophobia, but days before I went to this show, I saw teenage Asian girls in Koreatown wearing his merch. No matter what homophobes say to him, he's going to be more than fine.

But with Santana's rise, it was nice to see that there truly could be more than one. They are not the first queer Black artists, but these were the first I saw be embraced by wider audiences.

When I first discovered him on Instagram via Caresha from City Girls, he looked exactly like most of the people I met in gay clubs across the South. He reminds me of so many of my brother's friends. He reminds me of friends I made through my brother through our time spent together at the clubs.

Santana reminds me of home in that way, but that also brings attention to how often those kinds of gay men are hidden or not allowed to flourish for being too this, too that, blah-blah-blah. I had already found Santana to be a good rapper noticeably improving with each project, but I had never seen him perform. Proud as

I was of Big Latto, my friend Kristian, who came with us, tapped me to say how surreal it was to see a sold-out crowd rap a gay Black boy's music word for word.

"I never thought this day would come."

Come to think of it, neither did I.

Yet there we were, watching him command the crowd and be brought out multiple times by Lattto to perform during her set. The City Girls performed with Latto, and after I literally rapped every damn line from their song "In n Out," they stayed onstage with Santana. To perform with him and, as I turned my eyes to them afterward, watch him flourish.

You could see how happy they were for him.

I was, too, and for the people like us.

I saw him some months later perform at a Summer Walker concert with the whole arena in his favor.

I was beginning to let that dream go, but I may never have absolute peace until I release some kind of mixtape. I'll be the oldest gay rapper in the world, but if it happens, I'll be grateful to folks like Santana for paving the way for me.

As long as I stay awake, anything can happen.

<hr />

While I came to LA with the right attitude, I was a different person. Someone far more exhausted than I ever remember being. Someone struggling with a combination of depression, grief, and rampant anxiety.

For a while, the only reprise from it was going to bed early.

Initially, my sleep pattern was off after juggling so many time zones over the past several months.

Now the issue was me.

I have liked some "old-people things" since I was a kid.

Say, watching the news, complaining about taxes, eating early.

But this early-bird-special bedtime was not what I envisioned for myself or the last of my thirties.

I wouldn't say my party days are over. They are different in that I'm more selective. But in this case, I wasn't just not partying. I stopped doing much of anything.

There were new health scares among loved ones. There was more stress and pressure from work. Everything was more expensive than I remembered. Doing anything felt overwhelming after a while.

I found myself not only stagnant socially, but somewhat stymied creatively.

Usually, in moments of great doubt, my favorite Creole, Beyoncé, will resurface and remind me to stop acting so pitiful.

It usually does the trick, but when she released her new single, "BREAK MY SOUL," I did not love the song.

"That's why you're never being sent an Ivy Park box" was the first text response I received when I shared the news.

I never thought the song, which samples the early nineties hit "Show Me Love" by Robin S and features vocals from Big Freedia, was bad. It's not that I don't like or appreciate house music. When I heard rumors of Beyoncé going back to more up-tempo tunes on her new album, my mind immediately raced to *B'Day*. I was hoping for songs like "Kitty Kat," "Suga Mama," "Get Me Bodied," or "Freakum Dress."

Or her living up to my dreams of her releasing a rap album.

I don't care what some of y'all say about Beyoncé the rapper, but she's one of the greatest rappers of all time as far as I'm concerned.

So is Mariah Carey.

This song wasn't that.

My initial reaction was that the song was more or less an auntie version of Destiny's Child's "Happy Face."

When I first heard that song on Destiny's Child's *Survivor*, I found it so corny.

Someone told me that I had been referred to as a "cute curmudgeon," and it's sentiments like this that I imagine all but confirm the categorization.

After the single release, I lowered my expectations for the album.

Not to say she wouldn't produce a good album, but perhaps in her forties, she might be getting safer on me.

Obviously, depression and grief had me thinking like a damn fool.

I can't recall who tweeted it, so pardon my paraphrasing of it, but of all the initial reactions to Beyoncé's seventh studio album, *Renaissance*, my favorite is the quip that it's a record for "middle-aged gay men and Black women who post Issa Rae memes."

Whoever wrote the above tweet might have issued that review pejoratively, but those with taste know better. Beyoncé makes music for the masses, but she's always done it with a point of view and with a core fan base in mind. This is especially true of me—an aging millennial still affectionately referring to her as "My Lord and Gyrator." And I will until the day she personally tells me to stop.

Renaissance turned out to be remarkable in every measure and was every bit the up-tempo album I wanted, only better than I could have predicted.

In liner notes posted on her website, Beyoncé writes that *Renaissance* is intended as a "safe place, a place without judgment . . . a place to be free of perfectionism and overthinking."

Ah, it's an album for people like me to remember to relax and bop and sing along.

Can I stan for a bit?

There are still plenty of references on this album to the social and political issues of our time, and I love that, but I love more that they exist within a sea of samples, interpolations, live instrumentation, and sounds ranging from disco and house to funk, Afrobeat, dancehall, ballroom, and techno.

Renaissance is, above all, a dance album—one that tries to capture the breadth and diversity of Black music and people. It features Grace Jones and Nile Rodgers, the Atlanta rapper Kilo Ali, Chicago house artist Lidell Townsell, and other contributors ranging from Syd to Drake to Sabrina Claudio. Ever Southern and self-affirming, only Beyoncé could mix gospel legend Twinkie Clark and bounce artist DJ Jimi to make an ass-throwing anthem called "CHURCH GIRL" that doesn't feel sacrilegious.

Then there is my obsession, "PURE/HONEY," which samples multiple club hits: Kevin Aviance's "Cunty," Moi Renee's "Miss Honey" and MikeQ's "Feels Like." I love when this woman releases music that directly locates the sugar in my tank. She always snapped for the kids, but this is her gayest album to date. And unlike some, I mean that in the best way.

I am addicted to "AMERICA HAS A PROBLEM."

I love just about every song minus "THIQUE" (sorry), but bottom line, no song on the record sounds like another, yet they fit perfectly as a collection. All of the transitions are seamless, and in hindsight, I may not have been the biggest fan of "BREAK MY SOUL," but hearing it after "ENERGY" and along with the rest of the album, I understand it better as a first single.

What a fool I was to doubt her.

In an *open letter* released in tandem with the album, Beyoncé dedicated *Renaissance* to the LGBTQ+ community as a whole, and in particular to her uncle Johnny, her gay uncle who died of AIDS.

"He was my godmother and the first person to expose me to a lot of the music and culture that serve as inspiration for this album," Beyoncé wrote. "Thank you to all of the pioneers who originate culture, to all of the fallen angels whose contributions have gone unrecognized for far too long. This is a celebration for you."

I lost an uncle to AIDS, and so I understand that a lot of men like Uncle Johnny—men like me—were taken too soon.

The fact that *Renaissance* is dedicated to Johnny, and the community he belonged to, speaks to the underlying optimism found throughout the album.

Many of them didn't even get to make it to their fourth decade.

What a privilege it is for me to be alive to see this sea change in the wake of lingering opposition.

That album renewed a sense of optimism in me.

It reminded me that my best years remain in front of me.

Part of my moving to LA was recalling the first time I lived here and noticing how many people in their forties and fifties carried themselves in ways considered "youthful." As in active but not, like . . . a try-hard. And they looked good. I couldn't tell a lot of their ages back when I hung with some of them back in my twenties. Some of that could have been cosmetic boosts, but most of their faces gave off health and happiness—okay, and money, too.

Ultimately, this is a nice place for me to grow older and remain feeling full of life—as long as I make the choice to.

I keep being told that once I hit forty, I'll feel a lot lighter. That my perspective will change. That I'll be more settled into myself.

I feel like I am closer. I wish the last few years were easier, but all I can do now is be grateful that I have survived them with my spirit shaken but intact.

The friend who told me to shut up and just turn Beyoncé on had a point. I wasn't ready for it at the time.

That and the "BREAK MY SOUL" remix with Madonna is better.

Either way, I'm glad I got the message of the song now.

The lessons I got from her and the album—that I still fit, that I can still create, that there is still so much joy and life to have, no matter the age—are worth it.

I should have never doubted Beyoncé, but she did get me back. When it was time to buy *Renaissance* tour tickets, I never got a code from Ticketmaster.

I don't worry about it, though.

I'll get where I need to be.

I always do.

Acknowledgments

My mama, my heart and my sun, was diagnosed with cancer as I struggled to overcome the grief that was already dragging me down while struggling to finally finish this book.

She fought so hard, but regrettably cancer stole my favorite person in the world. I am heartbroken and words that don't begin and end with the pain I feel escape me, but I do want to at least say thank you to every single person that has supported me in any way in 2023, which I can now say has been the worst year of my life.

And thank you to anyone trying to help me fill the home in my heart from now until I'm gone myself.

I will figure it out, but before my mama passed on, she told me she was proud of me. I will put that energy into keeping my dream alive for her, my guardian angel.

About the Author

Michael Arceneaux is the *New York Times* bestselling author of *I Can't Date Jesus* and *I Don't Want to Die Poor*. He is currently doing the best with what he's got in Los Angeles.